MW00753873

LOVE
IS
SERVED

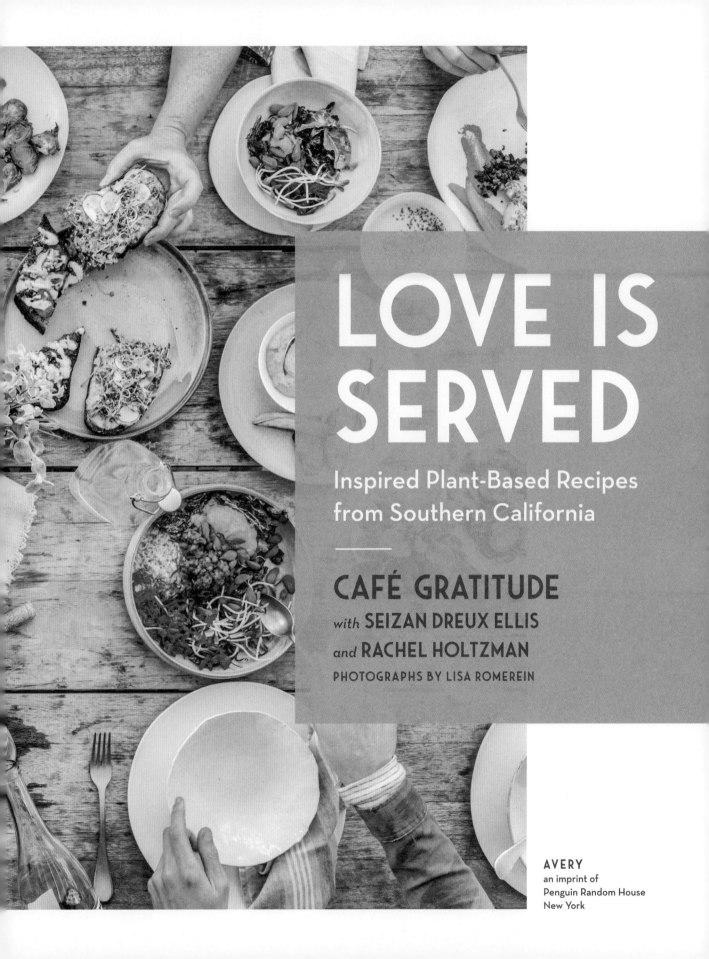

LOVE IS SERVED

Inspired Plant-Based Recipes
from Southern California

CAFÉ GRATITUDE

with **SEIZAN DREUX ELLIS**
and **RACHEL HOLTZMAN**

PHOTOGRAPHS BY LISA ROMEREIN

AVERY
an imprint of
Penguin Random House
New York

AVERY

an imprint of Penguin Random House LLC
penguinrandomhouse.com

Copyright © 2020 by Dreux Ellis
Photographs by Lisa Romerein
Photographs by Eric Wolfinger: pages 12–13, top middle, lower far left,
lower right, and lower far right

Penguin supports copyright. Copyright fuels creativity, encourages
diverse voices, promotes free speech, and creates a vibrant culture.
Thank you for buying an authorized edition of this book and for
complying with copyright laws by not reproducing, scanning, or
distributing any part of it in any form without permission. You are
supporting writers and allowing Penguin to continue to publish books
for every reader.

Most Avery books are available at special quantity discounts for bulk
purchase for sales promotions, premiums, fund-raising, and educational
needs. Special books or book excerpts also can be created to fit specific
needs. For details, write SpecialMarkets@penguinrandomhouse.com.

Library of Congress Cataloging-in-Publication Data
Names: Dreux Ellis, Seizan, author. | Holtzman, Rachel, author.
Title: Love is served : inspired plant-based recipes from Southern
    California / with Seizan Dreux Ellis and Rachel Holtzman.
Description: New York : Avery, an imprint of Penguin Random House,
    2020. | Includes index. | Summary: "Bright, clean, and hip recipes to
    enchant vegans, vegetarians, and omnivores alike, from plant-based
    haven Café Gratitude"— Provided by publisher.
Identifiers: LCCN 2019029956 (print) | LCCN 2019029957 (ebook) |
    ISBN 9780525540052 (hardcover) | ISBN 9780525540069
    (ebook)
Subjects: LCSH: Vegetarian cooking. | Cooking, American—California
    style.
Classification: LCC TX837 .D74 2020 (print) | LCC TX837 (ebook) |
    DDC 641.5/636—dc23
LC record available at https://lccn.loc.gov/2019029956
LC ebook record available at https://lccn.loc.gov/2019029957
p.   cm.

Printed in China
10 9 8 7 6 5 4 3 2 1

Book design by Ashley Tucker

The recipes contained in this book have been created for the
ingredients and techniques indicated. The Publisher is not responsible
for your specific health or allergy needs that may require supervision.
Nor is the Publisher responsible for any adverse reactions you may
have to the recipes contained in the book, whether you follow them as
written or modify them to suit your personal dietary needs or tastes.

To all of our guests, past and future,
for whom we have eternal gratitude

Café Gratitude began with a very simple mission: to serve as a gathering place—one where people could walk in feeling instantly accepted, discover a path to elevate their perspective on life, and connect with a like-minded community. That goal didn't necessarily include having six locations throughout California, almost daily celebrity sightings, and a devout following of customers who treat our restaurants as an extension of their own kitchens and homes. But over the last seven years, that's what our company has miraculously witnessed. While we of course owe much of that success to Chef Seizan Dreux Ellis's inspired and enlightened plant-based offerings using ingredients that are just as kind to the Earth as they are to our bodies, we also trace these accomplishments to our humble and most dependable guides: love and gratitude. They are what permeate our culture, from the people who grow our food, to those who prepare and serve it, and to those who eat it. They are what inform our choices as a company, whether it's supporting regenerative agriculture, consistently finding new ways to leave a smaller footprint on our planet, or serving foods that function as both indulgence and medicine. They are what saw us through the evolution from a small raw food café in San Francisco to an internationally recognized restaurant group. They were the beacons that fascinated Chef Dreux and allowed him to fill our menu with dishes that energize, comfort, and inspire; and they are what have knit a community from the millions of people who have graciously allowed us to serve them.

But to us, success is not just measured by tables filled or by anyone entering our spaces feeling welcome, appreciated, and satisfied. We believe that the true success of our mission is when these same individuals go out into the world ready to pass on those exceptional feelings. And so a more beautiful world is made. Now we're passing on that love and gratitude to you, in the form of this book and our most treasured recipes that we've served over the years. Our food is just as much about spirit as it is about appetite, so we invite you to welcome these recipes into your own home and, in turn, create and share the abundance.

OUR EVOLUTION

Café Gratitude's founders, Matthew and Terces Engelhart, have always believed that given an open, supportive, and loving environment, people could be inspired to transform their lives. They also believe that changing your outlook and, in turn, your life, begins with a focus on gratitude—and that each of us has much to be grateful for, no matter our circumstances. To their minds, turning our attention from what we *don't have* to *all that we have been given* is a foundation for meaningful human growth. Although they weren't necessarily looking to open a restaurant as the encapsulation of these ideas, that's exactly what they did. The first Café Gratitude opened in 2004 in the Mission District of San Francisco. They served 100 percent plant-based, organic, from-scratch, raw foods—being among the first in this country to do so. They coupled that with the concept of Sacred Commerce, or the philosophy that a functioning business can also be a place of empowerment, giving employees—or advocates, as they are referred to—a place to feel heard and appreciated. The idea was that this acknowledgment would be passed on to the customers, who in turn would feel nourished, both physically and emotionally, and bring that feeling with them out into the world. Matthew and Terces planted the seed that love is a contagious way of being.

In 2011, Terces and Matthew partnered with CEO Lisa Bonbright and her husband, Chris, to bring Café Gratitude 2.0 to Southern California. Along with the Engelharts' adult children, Cary and Ryland—now our chief operations officer and chief inspiration officer, respectively—the team opened our first Los Angeles restaurant in Larchmont Village. Over the next seven years, our company Love Serve Remember opened five more locations, in Venice, the Arts District in downtown Los Angeles, Beverly Hills, San Diego, and Newport Beach. But despite our growth, our core values and mission have remained the same.

Chef Seizan Dreux Ellis joined the endeavor in 2008 to open more hearts and minds to plant-based food. After helping the Engelharts and Chef Chandra Gilbert (now the executive chef at our sister restaurant Gracias Madre) deliver their vision in the Bay Area, he stepped into the role of executive chef in Los Angeles in 2011. While still honoring the founding principles of Café Gratitude, Chef Ellis expanded and evolved the menu to include cooked foods in addition to some of the beloved original raw offerings (including the then-trailblazing selection of raw desserts—Gratitude classics that have never come off our menu for fear of revolt, and are included in this book). He brought with him a deep understanding of how to celebrate the flavors of plants in their most natural state, while also creating dishes that scratch the deepest of indulgent itches for vegans, vegetarians, and omnivores alike. But no matter how seemingly naughty—cinnamon rolls, "chicken-fried" oyster mushrooms and waffles, eggplant Parmesan, mole abuelita enchiladas, Black Lava Cake—each of these offerings call for organic, from-scratch, healing, and healthful ingredients free of animal products, processed soy, and in almost all cases, refined sweeteners. Testament to just how inventive, satisfying, and full flavored the food is: only 20 percent of our customers are vegetarian or vegan.

Throughout the growth of Café Gratitude, there is one thread that has continued to firmly connect us to our founding principles: our affirmations and Questions of the Day. Looking at our menu—and through this book—you'll notice that each dish has its own unique pronouncement: "I Am Thriving," "I Am Open-Hearted," "I Am Powerful." These affirmations have been a part of the Gratitude culture since day one and are a special part of the transformative process. There's something subtle yet powerful that happens when you say to your server, "I am Serene," and they then say back to you, "You are Serene." It's then repeated as the server passes the order on to the kitchen, back to the server as the order is ready, and again to you. It's a series of simple moments that manage to create a tangible energetic shift, and it's a reflection of one of our guiding truths: You are nourished just as much by your food as you are by your thoughts. The same goes for the Question of the Day, which our servers share with our guests if they're interested in receiving it. "What's something that brought you joy today?" "What are you afraid of?" "What are you most grateful for?" Our guests are invited to discuss among themselves, and it's an opportunity to open and reflect. If you're interested in creating that space in your own home, we've included both our signature affirmations as well as some sample Questions of the Day throughout the book. We encourage you to take a moment before your meal—whether it's just you or a gathering of family and friends—to consider the question, share your findings, and say aloud the affirmation. Should you not want to partake, we assure you that your food will be every bit as soul-stirring as it is delicious.

Our goal for this book is to bring the expression of love from our restaurants into your home. Eating living, plant-based foods has had a profound effect on all of our lives, which we want to extend to you. It's also challenged us to find new, delectable ways to share these plants. This book is the culmination of that effort, offering you the ability to make Gratitude-quality food in your own kitchen. The dishes you'll find here are handpicked, first and foremost, because they are Café Gratitude favorites. They are recipes that our guests have grown to crave over the years and have requested time and time again. We've taken care to make them as home cook-friendly as possible while still staying true to the from-scratch essence of our food. They are recipes for all day, every day, featuring easy-to-access, easy-to-use ingredients. We've also included a few more challenging recipes for special occasions and gatherings, though nothing we won't help see you through. We invite you to play with these recipes, dabbling with individual sauces, dressings, or cheeses; making them your own and tailoring them to your tastes and preferences. We are honored to be a part of your journey and wish you fulfilling, delicious success!

LISA BONBRIGHT, CEO

The first time I stepped into Café Gratitude was in 2007. I had gone up to San Francisco to move my in-laws into their new condo, and my plan was to spend those two child-free, husband-free weeks taking really good care of myself—hiking Mount Tamalpais every day and eating well. I've always valued my health, especially during my pregnancies with my two girls, and at this point in my life I was interested in raw food. I asked a friend where I should go, and she said, "You gotta try this place in San Rafael called Café Gratitude." So I showed up when they opened for breakfast. It's hard to describe what I felt when I walked in—almost as though I had finally found a community that I didn't even realize I had been looking for all my life. I can still distinctly remember the smell—like fresh juice and greens. I sat down and the server asked me the Question of the Day, and I'll admit it made me uncomfortable at first. I had never really eaten alone, and I wasn't sure if there was a right or wrong answer. But the server—or advocate, as I later came to know they were called—was nonjudgmental and accepting. And on top of that, completely knowledgeable and passionate about healthy food. There was cold-brewed coffee, cold-pressed juices, and turmeric lattes with almond milk—this was eleven years ago! No one knew what those things were back then. I saw people coming in to fill their jugs of alkaline water—something I'd never heard of before that point—and there was a small retail section that was loaded with fascinating-looking books and supplements the café's owners recommended, which you could easily spend an afternoon perusing. It was just this plethora of wellness. But most important, someone had finally figured out how to make raw vegan food delicious. I decided then and there that this was what I wanted my lifestyle to be and ended up eating every meal there for the next ten days. At that point I called my husband, Chris—who is in commercial real estate—and told him that we had to find out who the owners were because I wanted to broker a deal and get them down to Los Angeles. To which he said, "Either you've lost your mind or you're on to something really big."

When Chris brought our girls up to San Francisco to visit their grandparents in their new condo, I took them straight from the airport to Café Gratitude. I had called ahead and had a table set up for them, filled with smoothies, savory dishes like enchiladas, and house-made raw chocolates. Everyone could see exactly what I had been talking about. Meanwhile I was driving my husband nuts asking whether he'd tracked down the owners. (If I get myself excited about something, forget it.) This went on for about two weeks until Chris said he hadn't been able to get a response. So at my urging, we poured our hearts into a letter, telling the owners how we felt about their business and how passionate we were about bringing it to Southern California. We overnighted it and got a call the next day, asking whether we wanted to come up for a meeting. I was a nervous wreck—and I don't really get nervous. But we walked into Gratitude's central kitchen, and there were Matthew and Terces. The four of us hit it off as though we'd been friends our entire lives. We talked for four hours that afternoon, discussing what our plan could look like. Over the next six months, they'd come visit us in L.A., or we'd drive up to their biodynamic Be Love Farm in Vacaville, and we'd all spend time together, including their two sons, Ryland and Cary. We'd sit around a roaring fire outside their yurt at 8 a.m., drinking fresh-pressed wheatgrass juice, and just dug deep. Matthew and Terces really knew how to communicate and how to explore topics that got to the core of person-to-person connection. At first it was uncomfortable being close to that kind of radical honesty, but then I quickly realized how freeing it could be. We'd have long conversations about things like transformation and Sacred Commerce, getting to know one another on a deeper and deeper level. And while we were very much opposites in many ways, we were also so much alike.

> My mission has been to change the way people look at food and take care of their bodies.

But even after we'd grown a beautiful friendship, it still wasn't clear what the next steps would be in terms of bringing Café Gratitude to L.A. Matthew and Terces eventually shared that they weren't looking to expand. They preferred to focus on their writing, lecturing, consulting, and farming versus increasing the footprint of the restaurants. Instead they invited us to partner with them in order to roll out Café Gratitude in Southern California. Well, in our family we have a golden rule: No investing in restaurants! Chris knew all too well from his experience in real estate that the restaurant industry was one of the hardest to find success in. So he told them, "We're not getting into the restaurant business, but let's stay friends." We shook hands and left.

But as we were driving home, I couldn't fight an overwhelming surge of frustration. I realized that I wanted this, even if Chris didn't. I launched an impassioned plea. "For the past twenty-five years, I've raised your kids," I told him. "I've managed your properties. I've attended every event, party, and award ceremony. I've supported you in everything you've wanted to do." And then I said, "You owe me. We're doing this." Chris almost veered off the road, he was so surprised! He knew I meant it, and said, "I'll tell you what I'll do—I'll get all their finances; look under the hood." I think Chris had basically assumed that the numbers would kill the deal, and that he'd be able to shut me down. But when we got their financials, they were—quite honestly—off the hook. To give you some context, McDonald's as a benchmark does about $500 per square foot in sales. On average, Café Gratitude was doing more than double that. After that, I couldn't be stopped—I was on a mission.

We raised money among our friends, put in some of our own money, found a space in a building we owned in Larchmont, and got to work designing Gratitude 2.0. We wanted to take the culture and food from the Bay Area and rebrand Café Gratitude Larchmont as a modern vegan diner. We wanted to create a space where you could bring a date or host a special event—and just so happen to be eating truly healthy food. We opened our doors on March 4, 2011, and it was like lightning in a bottle. We had a line out the door with celebrities waiting with everyone else to get in—between eight hundred and nine hundred guests a day.

We managed to take the true, unadulterated spirit of the original Café Gratitude concept and apply a fresh, more modern take that would speak to an L.A. customer. And as the interiors became more elevated, so did the food. Thanks to Dreux, we successfully shifted to offering cooked food options while still embracing the sustainable, seasonal spirit of the menu. While I'm not a vegetarian or vegan, I do truly believe in the power of eating plants—and that you don't have to be punished for it. Chris used to say that eating plant-based food was like mowing the lawn and eating the grass—no flavor, no mouthfeel, and no presentation. But the Engelharts and Dreux have figured out how to make vegan food delicious. My mission has been to change the way people look at food and take care of their bodies, and making Café Gratitude an accessible, welcoming place to be has catalyzed that vision. As I like to say, Café Gratitude is changing the world one bite at a time.

SEIZAN DREUX ELLIS,
EXECUTIVE CHEF

I first heard about Café Gratitude—the Bay Area incarnation—in 2008. I was living and working in Venice, Italy, as a vegan chef, focusing on how to take the vast traditions of Italian food and translate them into vegan dishes. I'd actually moved to Italy on a grant to make experimental films, and I was supposed to be writing a script. Instead I found myself at the market every day, and in the kitchen. I also met a man, whose mother—and my eventual mother-in-law—was an amazing cook and mentor. She not only cooked for her family—including her eleven children— three meals a day for thirty years, but she also learned to cook in postwar Italy, in what they call *La Cucina Povera* ("the poor kitchen"). Out of necessity she taught herself to make meals that featured beans, grains, and fresh vegetables over more expensive and less available meat and dairy. She learned how to use toasted breadcrumbs in place of Parmesan, and capers instead of sardines. From her I got a solid education on how to make vegetarian food that was still satisfying, and most important, how to do so with love.

After a year of living in Italy, I had no film script, but I was coming to terms with my unvented passion to cook. So at the age of forty, I decided to become a chef. I started at the bottom, chopping onions in hotel kitchens, and worked my way up and into some Michelin-starred restaurants. I continued my apprenticeship with my mother-in-law and eventually opened a small organic vegetarian *gastronomia* (a deli counter, essentially, without the meat) in a working-class section of Venice.

Raw vegan cuisine was just starting to take off in the States, and I'd been following the opening of restaurants like Roxanne's in San Francisco and Pure Food and Wine in New York. Sometime in 2008 I was listening to a raw-food podcast and heard an interview with Matthew and Terces Engelhart. I was standing in the kitchen of the *gastronomia* at 5 a.m., peeling potatoes, listening to them talk about the raw-food community in the Bay Area, and crying. They were talking about the power of food to heal—not just people but the planet, which were ideas that I'd taken to heart since becoming an ethical vegan at nineteen. I was

19

also realizing the unsustainability of running a business in Italy on my own—I was doing everything from the food prep to the books—and I knew that I wanted to be a part of what they were building over there.

Leaving Italy after living there for nine years was the hardest thing I've ever done, but my heart told me it was the right decision. So I packed up my life in Venice and moved back to San Francisco. When I got there I heard through mutual friends that a colleague I'd worked with at Greens Restaurant (a vegetarian restaurant where I'd worked front-of-house many years prior) was running operations at Café Gratitude. (It turned out to be the aforementioned Chandra Gilbert.) All she had was a part-time position, but she said, "If you want to work here, take this job and see what happens." At the time, Café Gratitude was primarily raw food, so the restaurants didn't actually cook food; they just assembled it. Everything was prepared—chopped, pureed, dehydrated—in a central

> My approach has always been, "How can I serve you?"—just one manifestation of my path as a Zen Buddhist in my work.

commissary kitchen that supplied six restaurants in the Bay Area. We had one guy who worked an eight-hour shift just cracking coconuts, scooping out the meat for our coconut milk. So I started in the central kitchen as a part-time prep cook, then became the manager of the entire central kitchen, and eventually became the executive chef of all six Café Gratitude restaurants in Southern California.

When we opened the first Los Angeles restaurant in Larchmont, it was becoming clear that our customers were interested in cooked food as well as raw. The raw-food-only trend had started to die off, but the appetite for delicious vegan food was growing. While there are some chefs who say, "This is my vision, and this is what you must accept," my approach has always been, "How can I serve you?" It's just one manifestation of my path as a Zen Buddhist in my work. So when the time came to update the menu at Café Gratitude, I started with how I could best serve the community. We kept our food as close to the ground as possible—meaning whole plants in their least processed state—while also honoring seasonality. And, of course, I tapped into the lessons I learned in Italy, which were very much about the simplest primary ingredients, of the best possible quality, simply prepared. I developed new techniques and strategies to make things easier on the kitchen, and pared the food down to the fewest steps and least fussy preparations possible. My biggest challenge as a vegan chef was and continues to be building flavors, while at the same time making sure that the recipes don't become so complex that they're all over the place. As a vegan, what I don't enjoy about some plant-based restaurants is that the food is so complicated! I had to find a balance between the primal simplicity of the cooking I'd grown to love in Italy and the drive to keep things interesting and fresh. What I've learned is that it's all about finding the middle way—another Zen Buddhist teaching. Over time I've discovered a few go-to techniques that translate into many different dishes. (The Mushroom Carnitas [see page 175], for example, can replace meat in a taco, a bibimbap bowl, or a pulled pork sandwich.) That's also reflected in this book: Most of these recipes use overlapping building blocks and can be mixed and matched as you please. You'll see how if you put in a little time—to blacken tofu or marinate a mushroom mixture or whip up a dressing—you can have a salad, a bowl, and a snack from that initial work. That's how we set up the kitchen at the restaurant, and that's how you can get the most out of your time and ingredients at home.

SEASONAL MENU IDEAS

Cultured cheese plate
   w/ smoked beet 'ham'

Smoked beet tartine
   w/ horser. dish toasts

Cast Iron 9
   wrapp

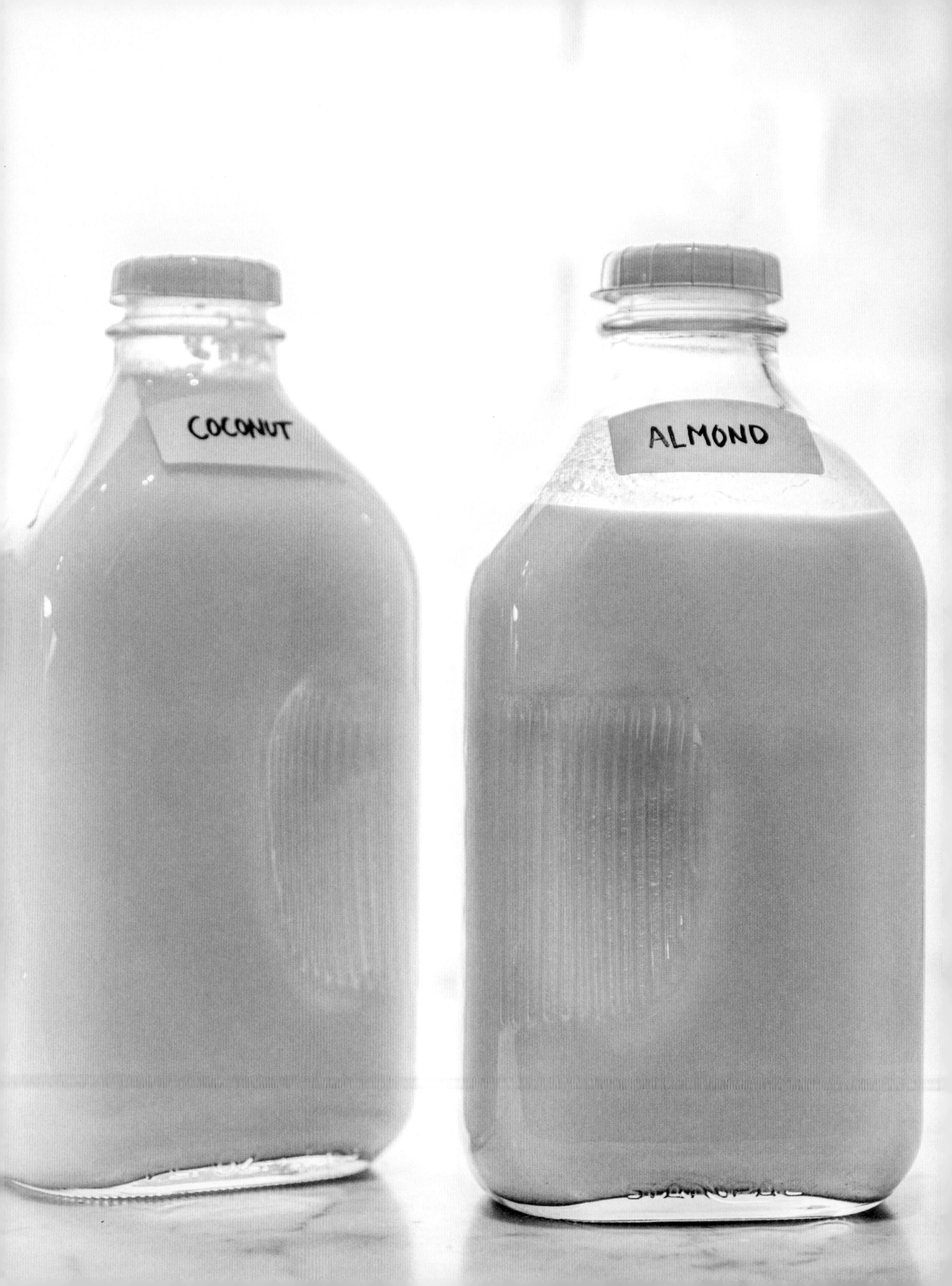
COCONUT
ALMOND

THE CAFÉ GRATITUDE PANTRY

When you cook from the ground up, beginning with the best possible fruits, vegetables, and other plants is paramount. That's why I strongly encourage you to seek out product from a local farmer who raises his or her produce with care—it makes a world of difference in the kitchen. And while you don't need to do much to great produce for it to be delicious, I've found that a small arsenal of kitchen staples—including seasoning mixes, milks, flours, and other plant-based blank canvases—in addition to the sauces, condiments, cheeses, and ferments in chapters 8 and 9—will expand your repertoire greatly. These are the workhorses of the Café Gratitude kitchen and are called upon with frequency, for good reason, throughout this book.

COMPASSIONATE BLEND

This flavorful paste is famous in our kitchens because it's a quick and easy way to bring a great salty, smoky, sweet note to any dish.

MAKES ABOUT 1 CUP

½ cup sun-dried tomatoes

¼ cup coconut oil, melted

2 tablespoons capers in brine, drained

1 tablespoon maple syrup

½ teaspoon smoked salt

1. In a medium bowl, soak the sun-dried tomatoes in hot water to cover for 15 minutes, until softened. Drain and reserve the soaking water.

2. In a blender, combine the soaked tomatoes, coconut oil, capers, maple syrup, and salt. Blend until a smooth, dense paste forms, adding a teaspoon or 2 of the tomato soaking water, if necessary. Transfer to a covered container and refrigerate for up to 2 weeks.

QUESTION *of the day* / What are you grateful for?

GOMASIO

Gomasio is a traditional Japanese sesame-seed seasoning that replaces salt with naturally salty sea vegetables. We use it in a number of our dishes, as it's delicious sprinkled on just about anything—soups, salads, roasted vegetables. This recipe comes from my treasured seaweed forager, Andrew Daunis, of Pacific Wildcraft, who has provided us with responsibly harvested Mendocino sea vegetables for many years. It calls for dried bull whip kelp fronds because they are very salty, and thus an excellent substitute for salt. The other advantage to using this kelp is that it is light and delicate and can be pulverized much more easily than other types of seaweed. However, other seaweeds can be used to make gomasio; it will just result in a different flavor and texture. The most important factor is that the seaweed is well dried for easy grinding.

MAKES ABOUT 5½ CUPS

3 ounces (about 4 cups) dried bull whip kelp fronds, or other seaweed of choice (wakame or hijiki work well)

1 cup organic black sesame seeds

2 ounces (scant ½ cup) pepitas

1. Place the kelp fronds in a high-speed blender with the speed set at medium-high; use the plunger or a spatula to push the seaweed along the sides of the blender jar into the center of the blender until all is well ground. Stop the machine and add the sesame and pumpkin seeds. Pulse the mixture 3 or 4 times until the desired consistency is reached. It should be a loose and dry mixture. If you blend the seeds too long, the mixture will quickly begin to resemble something more akin to tahini.

2. Store the gomasio in a container with a tight-fitting lid at room temperature for up to 1 month.

CHICKPEA EGG

At a certain point in building the Café Gratitude breakfast menu, I realized we didn't have an egg dish. Eggs for breakfast isn't exactly a Holy Grail of vegan cuisine, and because my approach is to use ingredients as close to the ground as possible, I didn't want to turn to processed or fake ingredients to simulate the real thing. Then I remembered from my years in Italy that they used *socca*, a chickpea (also called garbanzo bean) flour that's 100 percent protein and looks and acts like egg when whisked with water. The story goes that during a war between the Ligurians and the French back in the 1400s, there was a ship carrying garbanzo flour that was attacked, and crashed into the rocky outcroppings. The barrels of flour were soaked with salt water, but it was all the stranded sailors had to eat. They discovered that when it was spread out on the warm rocks and dried in the sun, it became this lovely salty, eggy kind of thing. To this day the Italians use it in various forms, including making a quiche-like dish called *farinata*. That's naturally what I referenced when I started thinking about how to create a quiche for our menu, and then again when I created our eggs Benedict and breakfast burrito. You could also just make the egg component, fry it up, and serve it as an antipasto or use it in a chopped salad for a hard-boiled egg effect.

MAKES ABOUT 1 CUP

1 cup garbanzo flour

1 tablespoon nutritional yeast

½ teaspoon kala namak salt or applewood smoked salt

¼ teaspoon ground turmeric

¼ teaspoon paprika

¼ teaspoon freshly ground black pepper

1 tablespoon tamari

¼ cup extra-virgin olive oil

1. In a medium bowl, whisk together the garbanzo flour, nutritional yeast, salt, turmeric, paprika, black pepper, tamari, and 1½ cups of water.

2. Heat 2 tablespoons of the oil in a large skillet over medium heat. Add half of the chickpea batter and gently work it around so it covers the entire pan in a thin, even layer. Allow the batter to cook almost completely on one side, barely 1 minute, then break it up with a spatula. Break it up and toss it a little to cook it evenly, nothing more. Work gently and let it cook without fussing with it too much or you will just end up with a paste. Transfer the chickpea egg to a plate. Heat the remaining 2 tablespoons of olive oil, add the other half of the batter, and repeat the cooking process.

TEMPEH CHORIZO

This recipe takes a traditional chorizo spice blend and simply replaces the animal proteins with the tempeh. It has a beautifully authentic flavor that really makes this dish shine. Like a "real" chorizo, the spices are given time to settle and infuse into the tempeh, so it's best to make this component at least a day or two in advance. (If you are short on time, there are a number of quality tempeh or soy chorizo products available that could be substituted with great results.) You could either form this into patties or sauté as a crumble.

SERVES 4 TO 6

1 tablespoon paprika

1 tablespoon ancho or chipotle chili powder

1 teaspoon cumin seeds

½ teaspoon dried oregano

½ teaspoon dried thyme

½ teaspoon whole black peppercorns

½ teaspoon chili powder

¼ teaspoon coriander seeds

¼ teaspoon ground cinnamon

1 dried bay leaf

Pinch of ground cloves

2 teaspoons Himalayan sea salt, plus more for blanching

1 pound soybean tempeh

¼ cup apple cider vinegar

3 tablespoons extra-virgin olive oil

1 tablespoon chopped garlic

1. In a spice or coffee grinder, combine the paprika, ancho chili powder, cumin, oregano, thyme, peppercorns, chili powder, coriander, cinnamon, bay leaf, and cloves and blend until it is a fine powder. Set aside.

2. Bring a medium pot of water to a boil and season with a generous pinch of salt. Add the tempeh and blanch for 3 minutes. Set aside to cool.

3. Over a large bowl, break up the cooled tempeh with your hands and add the apple cider vinegar, 1 tablespoon of the olive oil, the garlic, and 2 teaspoons sea salt. Massage the tempeh for 2 minutes, until the ingredients are well incorporated and the tempeh has crumbled. Add in the spice mixture and continue massaging the tempeh for an additional 2 minutes, so the spices are fully absorbed. Cover and leave the tempeh chorizo to marinate in the refrigerator for a minimum of 8 hours, though it's even better when left to rest overnight so the flavors can blend together and soften the tempeh.

4. In a large sauté pan over medium-high heat, warm the remaining 2 tablespoons of olive oil. Add the tempeh chorizo and brown it for 5 to 7 minutes, turning it and breaking it up until it is nicely browned and crumbly.

ALMOND MILK AND ALMOND PULP

This simple nut milk is easy to fold into your practice if you're curious about making your own. It has richer flavor and creamier body than any store-bought version, not to mention none of the preservatives. It's also advantageous because of the sprouted nut pulp leftovers, which can be used in the same way as store-bought organic almond flour. We find ourselves with an abundance of nut pulp thanks to our in-house almond milk production, so we've found a way to use it in all manners of baking, especially as a base for our raw layer cakes. The pulp can be saved in the freezer until you're ready to use it.

MAKES 7 CUPS OF ALMOND MILK (AND 1 CUP OF PULP)

2 cups raw almonds, soaked overnight in plenty of water

2 Medjool dates, pitted (see Note)

¼ teaspoon Himalayan sea salt

1. Drain and rinse the almonds (and dates, if applicable).

2. In a blender, combine the almonds, dates, salt, and 6 cups of water. Blend for 2 to 3 minutes, until the almonds are very finely ground.

3. Pass the milk through a nut milk bag or cheesecloth set over a large bowl. Squeeze the pulp well to extract all of the liquid. Store the milk in the refrigerator in a covered container for up to 3 days. The pulp can be frozen until ready to use.

NOTE Some dates are drier than others. If yours fall into the dry category, feel free to soak them with the almonds.

COCONUT MILK

Commercial coconut milk will work just fine in any recipe that calls for it. But if you want to make it a touch more special, try using this old-school Café Gratitude method. We prefer using fresh organic young Thai coconuts for both the coconut water and meat, but you could also buy bottled coconut water and find frozen coconut meat—the milk will be delicious all the same.

If you are using fresh coconuts, you will probably need 2 young Thai coconuts. In many grocery stores you can now buy these with the tops already shaved off so you can drink the water on the spot with a straw. If you can find them prepared this way, go ahead and use them, as it makes the meat and water easy to extract. Otherwise, to open a young Thai coconut, the simplest way is to use the bottom edge of a large kitchen knife or a cleaver to cut a square lid on the top of the coconut and then lift it off. Pour the water through a fine-mesh strainer into a bowl or large measuring cup to filter out any bits of shell that may have splintered while you were cracking the coconut. Set the water aside and scoop out the coconut meat with a large spoon. The coconut meat will vary from coconut to coconut. It can range from soft and jelly-like with a light pink color to thick, mature meat that is brilliant white. All will work in this recipe, but be mindful that the more mature meat will require more time in the blender to break down. If you scrape off some of the inner shell while you are scooping out the coconut meat, just use a small paring knife to remove it from the meat.

MAKES ABOUT 5 CUPS

4 cups coconut water
(from 2 young Thai coconuts
or bottled)

¾ cup shredded dried coconut
or coconut chips

½ cup coconut meat

¼ teaspoon Himalayan sea salt

1. In a blender, combine 3 cups of the coconut water and the dried coconut and blend until smooth.

2. Using a nut milk bag or cheesecloth stretched over a medium bowl, pass the coconut mixture through the bag, making sure to squeeze the pulp well to extract as much of the water as possible. Set the resulting coconut milk aside while you prepare the coconut cream. Rinse out the blender.

3. In the blender, combine the remaining 1 cup of coconut water, the coconut meat, and salt. Blend on high speed until you have a thick, completely smooth coconut cream. Whisk the cream into the coconut milk and store in a covered container in the refrigerator for up to 5 days.

COCONUT YOGURT

This is a very fast and easy recipe that takes no time or special equipment to make but should be prepared a day in advance because the yogurt will need time to ferment. Using the coconut kefir as the fermentation agent gives you the same probiotic boost as a traditional yogurt. The fermentation will happen naturally, with the yogurt getting tangier the longer it sits. This is also a great all-purpose yogurt to use in sauces and dressings.

The young coconut meat you want for this recipe is usually found in young Thai coconuts, which are now readily available in many grocery stores and Asian markets. If you buy the whole coconuts, you will have the added benefit of the coconut water but will have to crack the coconuts yourself and scoop out the meat (see page 32). My recommendation is to search out the frozen fresh young coconut meat from either Thailand or Vietnam. It comes packaged in 1-pound bags and can be found in the freezer section of many well-known national grocery chains, Asian markets, or ordered online.

MAKES ABOUT 2 CUPS

1 pound young coconut meat, fresh or frozen and thawed

1 cup coconut kefir

¼ cup fresh lemon juice

¼ cup agave nectar, coconut nectar, or maple syrup

1 tablespoon coconut oil

1. In a blender, combine the coconut meat, kefir, lemon juice, sweetener, and coconut oil. Blend until the yogurt is completely smooth and creamy, about 1 minute. Adjust the consistency of the yogurt by adding up to 1 cup of water just a splash at a time; it should be creamy, not grainy. Depending on your coconut meat, you may need very little or all of the water.

2. Refrigerate the coconut yogurt in an airtight container until you are ready to use it, up to a week. You can enjoy it the next day and still reap the probiotic and tangy benefits owing to the kefir, and it will continue to ferment in the refrigerator.

GLUTEN-FREE ALL-PURPOSE BAKERY FLOUR BLEND

Not all gluten-free all-purpose flour is created equal, so when we started developing our bakery offerings, we quickly realized that some of the recipes wouldn't work with store-bought versions. That's why we developed this proprietary blend, which is used in every one of our restaurants. It's proven to be most reliable in our gluten-free baking, as well as convenient for using in any other gluten-free all-purpose flour applications.

MAKES 6 CUPS

2½ cups brown rice flour

2½ cups white rice flour

1 cup tapioca flour (sometimes called tapioca starch)

2 tablespoons baking soda

1 tablespoon baking powder

2¼ teaspoons guar gum

In a large bowl, sift the brown rice flour, white rice flour, tapioca flour, baking soda, baking powder, and guar gum together. Store in an airtight jar for up to 1 month. To extend the shelf-life further, store the blend in the freezer.

QUESTION *of the day* / What do you love about your body?

DATE PASTE

Date paste is a natural fruit-based sweetener that offers an excellent gentle alternative to honey and maple syrup. It's made with nothing but dates and water (or, if your dates are extra juicy, just dates), can be used in just about any application needing a touch of sweetness, and can last for months in the freezer. You can sometimes find a store-bought version, but it's difficult to come by and can be coated in rice flour, which is why I highly recommend making your own.

MAKES 1 CUP

20 pitted Medjool dates

1. Add the dates to a food processor. If your dates are on the dry side, add 2 tablespoons of warm water. If the dates are pretty juicy, hold off on the water for the moment.

2. Process the dates until they form a smooth paste. You can add up to a total of ¼ cup of water if needed, just do a tablespoon at a time to avoid diluting the paste unnecessarily. Store in an airtight container in the refrigerator for up to 2 weeks or freezer for up to 3 months.

BREAKFAST
& BAKERY

I AM CONTENT
Cast-Iron Chickpea Quiche with Toasted Almond Romesco and Cashew Ricotta

This version of quiche has a Spanish feel, with the traditional romesco, or roasted pepper sauce, but you can get creative. You could do a full Italian theme with a Sun-dried Tomato Pesto (page 303); a Mexican version could include sweet corn and Cilantro Pumpkin Seed Pesto (page 301) or Pico de Gallo (page 169). The variations are endless. The Cashew Mozzarella (page 312) is a very fine addition to the quiche if you have a little extra time. Even using the gremolata is flexible—you can simply substitute a generous amount of fresh chopped parsley. Note that the chickpea batter needs to sit 6 hours or overnight to come together; you can whip it up the night before and make the quiche the next morning.

SERVES 4 TO 6

2 cups garbanzo flour

3 tablespoons extra-virgin olive oil

1½ teaspoons Himalayan sea salt

¼ cup diced red onion

3 cups roughly chopped baby spinach

½ cup seeded and diced Roma tomatoes

16 Kalamata olives, pitted and roughly chopped

¼ cup Toasted Almond Romesco (page 292)

¼ cup Cashew Ricotta (page 311)

2 tablespoons Gremolata (page 293), plus more to sprinkle on the quiche

1. In a medium bowl, whisk the garbanzo flour with 3 cups of water. Cover with a clean dish towel and let sit in the refrigerator overnight or for at least 6 hours. Skim off any foam that has accumulated at the top and whisk in 1 tablespoon of the olive oil plus the salt.

2. Preheat the oven to 350°F.

3. Heat the remaining 2 tablespoons of oil in an 8-inch cast-iron skillet over medium heat. Add the onion and cook for 3 minutes, until the onion is softened and lightly browned. Add half of the chickpea batter and the spinach. Cook for 2 to 3 minutes without stirring, until the spinach is slightly wilted, then add the tomatoes and olives, distributing them evenly across the surface of the quiche. Add the remaining chickpea batter and finish with a liberal sprinkling—1 to 2 tablespoons—of gremolata.

recipe continues

4. Continue cooking the quiche for approximately 5 minutes, until you see the edges begin to solidify. Transfer the pan to the oven and bake for 40 to 45 minutes, until the quiche is a dark golden color and the center is firm to the touch. Let the quiche rest for 5 to 10 minutes before serving, as it will set up a little more as it cools. The cast-iron skillet will keep it nice and warm.

5. Drizzle the romesco and cashew ricotta over the top of the quiche along with a finishing sprinkle of gremolata. This dish is delicious at room temperature but it can also be reheated in the oven and used in sandwiches or as a topping on salads.

QUESTION *of the day* / What do you love about your family?

I AM FESTIVE
Chilaquiles with Black Mole Abuelita and Tempeh Chorizo

We have a rich base of great Mexican cooks in all of our kitchens, and we have a love of Mexican food in Southern California, so when looking for variety in our breakfast offerings, this dish seemed like an obvious addition. And there was no need for me to re-create the wheel—I just needed to go to any one of my talented line cooks and say, "Let's do chilaquiles," and they were able to bring an authentic cultural reference that I don't necessarily have (even if I think I do!). In these instances, my role is to be a mentor, and then add Gratitude touches such as Tempeh Chorizo, Roasted Tomatillo Sauce, and Black Mole Abuelita, plus a drizzle of our Cashew Crema. You could take a shortcut by sourcing any of these components already prepared from your grocery store, but they are worth the extra effort if you have the time. And while this is how we prepare the dish in our cafés, there are as many variations as there are ingredients. So feel free to play with it and make it work for you.

SERVES 4 TO 6

For the Tortilla Chips:
Rice bran oil or neutral oil of your choice, for frying

Ten 6-inch corn tortillas

½ teaspoon Himalayan sea salt or applewood smoked salt

To Assemble:
2 tablespoons extra-virgin olive oil

1 small garlic clove, finely chopped

4 cups stemmed and chopped Lacinato kale (about 1 bunch)

⅛ teaspoon Himalayan sea salt

1. Make the tortilla chips: Pour the rice bran oil into a heavy-bottomed pot to a depth of about 2 inches. Over medium-high heat, bring the oil to 375°F. If you don't have a thermometer, you can test the readiness of the oil by dropping in a small piece of corn tortilla. When it floats easily and is covered in foaming oil bubbles, you know you have the correct heat.

2. Cut the tortillas into 8 wedges each. Line a baking sheet or tray with paper towels and set it next to the burner. Working in small batches, fry the tortilla wedges, turning them frequently with a fork or slotted spoon so they are evenly golden, 2 to 3 minutes. Using a slotted spoon, transfer the chips to the tray and lightly sprinkle them with salt. Keep an eye on the oil between batches, making sure it comes back up to temperature before adding fresh tortilla wedges.

recipe and ingredients continue

1 recipe Roasted Tomatillo
Sauce (page 295)

Tempeh Chorizo (page 29)

Black Mole Abuelita
(page 285)

Cashew Crema (page 311)

¼ cup diced red onion

1 small handful of fresh cilantro
leaves, chopped

3. Assemble: Preheat the oven to 150°F and place a large ovenproof serving platter inside to keep warm.

4. In a large pot over medium heat, warm the olive oil. Add the garlic and heat it gently for 1 minute. Add the kale, season with the salt, and sauté for 2 to 3 minutes, lightly tossing it until wilted. Transfer the kale to a medium bowl and set aside.

5. Place the empty pot over medium-high heat and add the roasted tomatillo sauce. When the sauce begins to boil, add the tortilla chips. Once the tortilla chips are coated with the warm sauce, allow them to cook for another minute before transferring them to the warmed serving platter. Top with a layer of the tempeh chorizo and the sautéed kale.

6. Finish the platter with generous drizzles of the black mole abuelita and the cashew crema, and garnish with the onion and cilantro.

NOTE You can make your own chips here, or buy them if you're short on time. Unsalted chips work best, and you'll need 8 to 10 cups. But it is really easy to make your own, and they are so delicious when they are fresh and warm! At Café Gratitude we always use organic corn tortillas so we are confident that they are free of GMO corn. Our frying oil of choice is rice bran oil, as it's generally considered one of the healthier oils due to its content of vitamin E, ideal fatty acid balance, antioxidant capacity, and cholesterol-lowering abilities.

I AM NURTURED
Breakfast Burrito with Chickpea Scramble, Black Beans, Roasted Potatoes, and Mole Coloradito

This is really an entire Mexican-inspired breakfast rolled up in a burrito. Each of the elements is a star on its own and worth taking the time to prepare, and while it seems like there are a lot of components to make for one breakfast burrito, consider that each of these could be leftovers from a meal during the week. The beans make for great grain-bowl additions; the chickpea egg is just as at home under roasted vegetables or tossed into a Gratitude Bibimbap Bowl (page 190); and the mole is pretty much your go-to condiment for anything that could use a little extra chili flavor. That said, while this recipe lays out the process that we use in the cafés, feel free to make adjustments, such as using canned beans instead of dried (see Note) or omitting the Compassionate Blend—it's open to interpretation and improvisation, and of course, lots of hot sauce.

If you'd like to really make this dish special, turn it into a burrito mojado by draping it in colorful sauces that reference the red, white, and green of the Mexican flag: Roasted Tomatillo Sauce (page 295), Salsa Verde (page 297), and Cashew Crema (page 311).

MAKES 4 LARGE BURRITOS

For the Mexican Black Beans:
¼ cup extra-virgin olive oil
1 cup chopped yellow onion
1 small jalapeño, seeded and finely chopped
1 garlic clove, chopped
¼ cup Compassionate Blend (page 26)

1. Make the Mexican black beans: In a large, heavy-bottomed pot over medium-high heat, heat the olive oil until shimmering. Add the onion, jalapeño, and garlic and sauté until the onion has softened, about 5 minutes. Add the compassionate blend and cook for another 2 minutes.

2. Add the beans, cumin, and bay leaf and stir to combine, allowing the beans to warm through, about 1 minute. Add 8 cups of water and bring the beans to a boil. Reduce the heat to low and partially cover the pot, keeping the beans

recipe and ingredients continue

2 cups dried black beans, soaked overnight, drained, and rinsed (see Note)

½ teaspoon ground cumin

1 dried bay or avocado leaf (see Notes)

2 teaspoons Himalayan sea salt, plus more to taste

For the Roasted Potatoes:

2 pounds small potatoes (heirloom varieties like German Butterball, Purple Peruvian, or French Fingerling all work nicely), cut into 1-inch chunks or left whole, if small

2 tablespoons plus ¼ teaspoon Himalayan sea salt

½ teaspoon baking soda

2 tablespoons extra-virgin olive oil

1 teaspoon chopped fresh rosemary (optional)

To Assemble:

4 large (10- to 13-inch) whole-wheat tortillas

1 cup roughly chopped baby spinach

1 cup roughly chopped romaine lettuce

Chickpea Egg (page 28)

2 avocados, cubed

1 cup Escabeche (page 319), chopped

½ cup Mole Coloradito (page 287)

at a low simmer for 1 hour and 20 minutes. Add the salt and simmer for an additional 10 minutes. Taste and check for seasoning and doneness, adding more salt or simmering a few minutes longer, if necessary. Set aside.

3. Make the roasted potatoes: Preheat the oven to 400°F.

4. In a large saucepan over high heat, bring 8 cups of water to a boil. Add the potatoes, 2 tablespoons of the salt, and the baking soda.

5. Return the water to a boil, then reduce the heat to medium to maintain an active simmer. Cook the potatoes until they are almost but not quite fully cooked (you should be able to skewer the potatoes with a knife, but still with some resistance), about 10 minutes. Drain the potatoes thoroughly, shaking the colander to remove any excess water.

6. In a large mixing bowl, toss the potatoes with the olive oil. Sprinkle with the remaining ¼ teaspoon of salt and the rosemary, if using, and toss once more.

7. Spread the potatoes evenly over a baking sheet and roast until brown and crispy, about 40 minutes. Turn the potatoes and shake the pan a few times during the process to make sure they are evenly roasted.

8. Assemble the burritos: In a large skillet over medium-high heat, lightly toast each tortilla for about 1 minute on each side. (A slightly more fun way to do this—if you are the daring type and have a gas range—is to toast the tortilla directly over the open flame for 30 seconds at a time, flipping it frequently until the tortilla is softened.) Cover the toasted tortillas with a kitchen towel to keep them warm.

9. For large burritos, in the center of each tortilla layer ¼ cup spinach, ¼ cup romaine, ½ cup roasted potatoes, ¼ cup chickpea egg, ¼ cup black beans, several cubes of avocado, and 2 tablespoons of the chopped escabeche. Drizzle 2 tablespoons of mole coloradito on top of the filling.

10. Fold the bottom half of the tortilla up and over the top of the filling ingredients. Fold in the flaps on either end and tightly roll the tortilla into a classic burrito shape. Return the burrito to the warm skillet, seam-side down, to seal the burrito, 1 to 2 minutes. Serve as is, or if making a nourished burrito mojada, spoon roasted tomatillo sauce, salsa verde, and cashew crema over each burrito.

NOTES If you do choose to use canned beans in this recipe, use an unsalted brand and drain and rinse them well before use. You will also need to reduce the final cooking time by half.

Another great addition to this recipe, if you come across them, is avocado leaves, which impart a unique regional flavor to the beans. You can find them dried in many farmers markets, particularly in Southern California. Otherwise, a bay leaf will do the job.

I AM TRUSTING

Barbecue Tempeh Scramble with Seasonal Vegetables, Shiitake Mushrooms, Spinach, and Avocado

I decided early on that we wouldn't use mock meat or fake meat substitutes at Gratitude, but I did want to incorporate tempeh because it's a fermented soy food that has a lot of substantial health properties. It's also very flexible in terms of the flavors and textures it can take on (see Tempeh Chorizo on page 29 and Tempeh Bacon on page 56). I wanted to create a scramble of some kind to anchor the breakfast menu—since who doesn't love a hearty, seasonal vegetable-filled savory scramble?—and I once again looked toward tempeh to add a protein element. We gave it the jerk treatment, with a marinade and blackening spices for a smoky edge. I'm also a big fan of barbecue sauce, so that's exactly what I tossed it with, as well as some simply sautéed vegetables, and then I piled it on top of one of our beautiful sourdough gluten-free baguettes to sop up all the juices. The result is a staple dish that is appropriate just about any morning of the week.

SERVES 4

For the Blackened Jerk Tempeh:
Pinch of Himalayan sea salt

1 pound tempeh

½ cup roughly chopped white onion

1 small scallion (white and green parts)

1 small garlic clove

One 1-inch knob fresh ginger

1 small jalapeño, seeded

2 teaspoons coconut sugar

2 teaspoons dried thyme

2 teaspoons freshly ground black pepper

1. Make the blackened jerk tempeh: In a medium pot over medium-high heat, combine 4 cups of water and the salt and bring to a boil. Blanch the tempeh for 3 minutes, then transfer to a paper towel–lined plate to cool.

2. While the tempeh is cooling, prepare the marinade. In a blender, combine the onion, scallion, garlic, ginger, jalapeño, coconut sugar, thyme, black pepper, allspice, nutmeg, cayenne, lime juice, apple cider vinegar, tamari, olive oil, and 1 cup of water and blend until smooth.

3. Pierce the cooled tempeh a number of times with a fork so that it will absorb more of the marinade. Transfer the tempeh to a shallow dish or pan and pour over the jerk marinade.

recipe and ingredients continue

½ teaspoon ground allspice

⅛ teaspoon ground nutmeg

⅛ teaspoon cayenne pepper

2 tablespoons fresh lime juice

2 teaspoons apple cider vinegar

2 tablespoons tamari

2 tablespoons extra-virgin olive oil, plus more for frying

For the Blackening Spice Mix:
½ cup paprika

2 tablespoons smoked sea salt

2 tablespoons cayenne pepper

2 tablespoons ground chipotle powder

2 tablespoons dried thyme

2 tablespoons dried oregano

2 tablespoons freshly ground black pepper

For the Sautéed Vegetables:
2 tablespoons extra-virgin olive oil

1 garlic clove, smashed and chopped

6 cups chopped mixed vegetables (see Notes)

1 cup stemmed and sliced shiitake mushrooms or other all-season vegetable

Himalayan sea salt, to taste

¼ cup white wine (optional)

To Assemble:
4 cups lightly packed baby spinach

¼ cup Barbecue Sauce (page 307) or store-bought, plus more as needed

2 avocados, cubed

2 tablespoons chopped mixed fresh herbs such as basil, cilantro, chives, or scallion, for garnish

Grilled sourdough toast (optional)

Marinate the tempeh for at least 4 hours, covered, in the refrigerator, though 8 to 12 hours is recommended.

4. Lightly oil a large heavy-bottomed or cast-iron skillet and place it over medium-low heat.

5. Make the blackening spice mix: In a small bowl, combine the paprika, smoked salt, cayenne, and chipotle. Stir in the thyme, oregano, and black pepper.

6. Remove the tempeh from the marinade, allowing any excess marinade to drip away. Dredge the tempeh in the blackening spices on all sides so it is well coated. Place the tempeh in the warm skillet and allow it to blacken for 5 to 7 minutes, until the spices are literally blackened. Flip the tempeh over and repeat. Set aside.

7. Make the sautéed vegetables: Heat the olive oil in a large, heavy-bottomed skillet or wok over medium heat. Add the garlic and sauté until golden, about 1 minute.

8. Begin to add the prepped vegetables, starting with those that will need the most cooking time (i.e., tougher varieties such as winter squash and root vegetables). Turn them over in the garlic and olive oil, slowly adding all of the vegetables based on their thickness and cooking time. Cook the vegetables until they are all tender.

9. Add the mushrooms and salt the mixture to taste. Increase the heat to medium-high and stir-fry for 2 minutes. Sprinkle the white wine, if using, over the mixture and sauté for another minute, turning the vegetables over until the alcohol in the wine is cooked off. Turn off the heat.

10. Assemble: Crumble the blackened tempeh into the warm vegetables, stirring and turning to combine and using the residual heat of the pan to warm the tempeh. Add the baby spinach and continue turning the mixture over until the spinach is wilted. You can turn the flame on low if needed.

11. Add ¼ cup of barbecue sauce and stir to combine it thoroughly with the vegetables and tempeh. Taste before adding more. The exact quantity of barbecue sauce will depend on the vegetables you've chosen and how saucy you want the scramble to be. I like the vegetables to be lightly coated by the barbecue sauce but not overpowered by it.

12. Divide the scramble among 4 bowls and top with the avocado and herbs. Serve with bread, if desired.

NOTES Good all-season basics to use as a base here would be cauliflower, broccoli, zucchini, carrots, and bell peppers. Then bring some seasonality to the mix with vegetables like asparagus, artichokes, green beans, or sweet corn in the spring and summer, and Jerusalem artichokes, red chicory, and butternut squash in the winter months.

If you want to keep this dish on the lighter side flavorwise, you can skip both the jerk marinade and the blackening spice.

I AM HOSPITABLE
"Chicken-Fried" Oyster Mushrooms and Gluten-Free Oat Waffles with Sweet Cashew Butter

When it comes to writing our menus, we sometimes struggle with how to describe dishes that are based on preparations where animal proteins are traditionally used. But "chicken-fried" oyster mushrooms feels about the best way to relay how beautifully the fried mushrooms capture the sweet and savory essence of this soul food classic. The idea originally came about because I'd always wanted to interpret this dish for our menu, but I had trouble finding an acceptable substitute for the chicken. Then one day I was looking at the oyster mushrooms we have pretty much at all times because we use them for our signature Mushroom Carnitas (page 175), and I realized that they have the same shreddable quality as chicken. I used a straightforward approach with gluten-free flour, paprika, and salt, plus an easy almond milk and apple cider vinegar "buttermilk," and the result was immediate: Every single person, including all the cooks on the line, got it and loved it. Especially paired with our perfect (if I do say so myself) waffles, which include oats and all the heartwarming benefits that they bring to any dish they touch.

The sweet cashew butter is a real treat, but it does require that you prepare it the day before so that it can properly set up. It adds a rich, yet delicate note of maple to the waffles and has a beautiful consistency that is a little lighter than commercially prepared vegan butter or margarine.

SERVES 4

For the Sweet Cashew Butter:
⅓ cup raw cashews
2 tablespoons maple syrup
Pinch of Himalayan sea salt
¼ cup coconut oil

1. Make the sweet cashew butter: In a blender, combine the cashews, maple syrup, and salt with ½ cup of water. Blend until the mixture is completely smooth without a hint of graininess. Blending time will vary; if you have a high-speed blender, you will reduce blending time considerably. Don't worry if the mixture warms slightly as you blend. When the mixture is smooth and creamy, add the coconut oil

recipe and ingredients continue

For the Waffles:

4 cups Almond Milk
(page 30) or store-bought

1 tablespoon apple cider
vinegar

2½ cups Gluten-Free
All-Purpose Bakery Flour
Blend (page 34)

1 cup rolled oats (gluten-free,
if preferred)

1½ teaspoons baking powder

1 teaspoon orange zest

½ teaspoon ground cinnamon

⅛ teaspoon Himalayan sea salt

½ cup coconut oil, melted

For the "Chicken-Fried" Mushrooms:

1½ cups Almond Milk
(page 30) or store-bought

¾ cup apple cider vinegar

2 cups Gluten-Free All-Purpose
Bakery Flour Blend (page 34)
or all-purpose flour

2 tablespoons cornstarch

2 tablespoons nutritional yeast

¾ teaspoon Himalayan sea salt

¾ teaspoon cayenne pepper

¾ teaspoon onion powder

¾ teaspoon garlic powder

¾ teaspoon paprika

½ teaspoon freshly ground
black pepper

4 large clusters oyster
mushrooms (about 3 to
4 ounces each; see Note)

Rice bran oil or neutral oil of
your choice, for frying

Applewood smoked salt

For Serving:

Maple syrup, warmed

Orange wedges, for garnish
(optional)

and continue blending until the coconut oil is completely incorporated into the cashews. Transfer the butter to a covered container and allow the mixture to set up overnight in the refrigerator.

2. Make the waffles: In a medium bowl, combine the almond milk and apple cider vinegar and let it sit for 10 minutes to curdle. Making an almond "buttermilk" for the waffle batter adds a really nice tang to the flavor of the waffles, and the vinegar works with the baking powder as an egg substitute that makes the dough lighter.

3. In a medium bowl, combine the flour, oats, baking powder, orange zest, cinnamon, salt, and coconut oil. Add the almond buttermilk to the mixture and mix until just combined.

4. Follow your waffle maker's instruction manual to make the waffles. You can keep the cooked waffles warm in a 150° to 200°F oven while you are making the others, if desired. They can also be made in advance and warmed in a toaster or toaster oven when you are ready to serve them.

5. Make the "chicken-fried" mushrooms: In a small bowl, combine the almond milk and apple cider vinegar and set aside for 10 minutes to curdle.

6. In a medium bowl, mix together the flour, cornstarch, nutritional yeast, salt, cayenne, onion powder, garlic powder, paprika, and black pepper.

7. Keeping one hand "wet" to manage the milk side of the batter and the other hand "dry" to handle the flour side of the batter, dip a cluster of oyster mushrooms in the almond buttermilk with your wet hand. Let the excess milk drip away, then drop the soaked mushrooms into the flour mixture. Use your dry hand to dredge the mushrooms in the flour mixture until they are well coated. Shake off any extra flour and repeat the process by dipping the mushrooms in the buttermilk a second time and finishing once again in the flour dredge. (Double-battering ensures a nice, crunchy breading on the mushrooms.) Set the battered mushrooms on the baking sheet or plate. Repeat with the remaining clusters of mushrooms.

NOTE In the ingredient list, I mention a "cluster" of oyster mushrooms. This is because these mushrooms are generally grown in clusters, and for this recipe it is best if you can keep a nice handful-sized bunch of them together for breading. If they break apart into 2 or 3 smaller clusters, that is fine, too. I just love the visual impact of that large bunch of fried mushrooms on top of the waffles.

8. Line a baking sheet or plate with paper towels and set it next to your frying station. In a deep cast-iron pan or heavy-bottomed pot over medium heat, add about 2 inches of oil. If you have a thermometer, look for an oil temperature of 350° to 375°F. You can also test the oil by dropping in a small crust of bread. When it is covered by small rolling bubbles and floats, the oil is ready. If you are doing a couple of batches of these—something I would highly suggest because they're that good—be sure to bring the oil back up to temperature between batches.

9. Drop the oyster mushroom clusters into the hot oil and let them fry for 3 to 5 minutes, until they are a dark, golden-brown color. If you're nervous or unsure, err on a longer cooking time. Transfer the cooked mushrooms to the paper towel-lined baking sheet or plate and sprinkle them with smoked salt.

10. To serve: If necessary, warm the waffles in the oven or toast them in a toaster. It is also a nice touch to warm the maple syrup. Plate the warmed waffles and top with the fried mushrooms. Smear a small dollop of the sweet cashew butter on the side. A nice orange wedge is a fun, vintage diner way to finish the dish.

I AM CELEBRATING

Gratitude Spinach and Asparagus Benedict with Chickpea Egg, Tempeh Bacon, and Macadamia-Cashew Hollandaise

This is the showpiece of the Gratitude brunch menu. It's the big-impact getter, the showstopper. But it's actually a very straightforward preparation of simple ingredients: salty, smoky tempeh bacon; sautéed seasonal vegetables; and our signature chickpea frittata, plus a one-blender recipe for hollandaise sauce and store-bought English muffins, bagels, gluten-free toast, or even butter lettuce cups. It is the ultimate Sunday morning, having friends over, and doing-it-up-right kind of experience.

That said, it will require a little planning, but you will be rewarded for your efforts. You can make the hollandaise and the eggs up to 3 days in advance. (In fact, the eggs are best made ahead, though you could use them right away if you are in a pinch.) The tempeh bacon is easy to make and really captures the maple smokiness that we associate with bacon. But if you want to save a little time, there is now a wide selection of vegan bacon products on the market that you can easily find in many grocery stores. Choose your battles and decide whether you will make everything from scratch as we do, or bring in some quality, store-bought elements. It will be delicious whichever choice you make.

SERVES 4

For the Tempeh Bacon:
Pinch of Himalayan sea salt

One 8-ounce block of tempeh (we use soybean)

½ cup maple syrup

¼ cup Barbecue Sauce (page 307) or store-bought

1 tablespoon paprika

1 teaspoon liquid smoke

1. Make the tempeh bacon: Line a plate with paper towels. In a medium pot over medium-high heat, combine 4 cups of water and the salt and bring to a boil. Blanch the tempeh for 3 minutes (this will help remove its fermented flavor), then transfer to the paper towel–lined plate to cool.

2. While the tempeh is cooling, prepare the marinade. In a medium bowl, whisk together the maple syrup, barbecue sauce, paprika, and liquid smoke.

recipe and ingredients continue

For the Macadamia-Cashew Hollandaise:

1⅓ cups raw macadamia nuts, soaked for 4 to 6 hours

⅓ cup raw cashews, soaked for 4 to 6 hours

2 cups Almond Milk (page 30) or store-bought

¼ cup extra-virgin olive oil

2 tablespoons coconut oil, melted

2 tablespoons fresh lemon juice

2 teaspoons apple cider vinegar

2 tablespoons nutritional yeast

1 teaspoon Himalayan sea salt

1 teaspoon Gremolata (page 293) or chopped fresh parsley

½ teaspoon Dijon mustard

⅛ teaspoon ground turmeric

To Assemble:

Chickpea Egg (page 28)

16 medium asparagus spears

½ teaspoon Himalayan sea salt, plus more to taste

1 tablespoon plus 1 teaspoon extra-virgin olive oil

8 packed cups baby spinach

2 vegan English muffins, split (or bread of your choice) or butter lettuce cups

½ cup Barbecue Sauce (page 307) or store-bought, plus more to taste

Gremolata (page 293) or chopped fresh parsley

Freshly ground black pepper

Roasted Potatoes (page 46) or a simple green salad

3. Cut the tempeh along the short end into ¼-inch-thick strips. In a shallow dish or pan, lay the tempeh strips in a single layer and cover them with the marinade. Let the tempeh marinate in the refrigerator for 8 to 12 hours.

4. Preheat the oven to 400°F.

5. Line a baking sheet with parchment paper and transfer the marinated tempeh strips to the baking sheet, leaving enough space for the strips to dry easily. Save whatever marinade is left over, as you can use it for at least 2 batches of tempeh. (It also makes an excellent vegetable marinade.)

6. Bake the tempeh for 5 to 6 minutes, until it looks halfway dried. Turn the strips and bake for an additional 3 to 4 minutes, keeping an eye on the bacon to make sure it doesn't dry out too much. It should be dry enough to be a little chewy, with a rich punch of flavor, but not dry or crunchy. It will also dry a little further as it cools. The bacon can be stored in the refrigerator for up to 1 week.

7. Make the macadamia-cashew hollandaise: Drain and rinse the nuts and transfer them to a blender. Add the almond milk, olive oil, coconut oil, lemon juice, apple cider vinegar, nutritional yeast, salt, gremolata or parsley, Dijon mustard, and turmeric plus ⅓ cup of water. Blend until the sauce is smooth and velvety. This may take longer with a regular blender but wait it out! The sauce should have the consistency of a thick cream. Don't worry if it seems a little thinner than a traditional hollandaise, as it will thicken somewhat when you heat it for plating. Set aside to use now or store in the refrigerator for up to 3 days.

8. Assemble the benedict: Preheat the oven to the lowest setting and place a baking sheet inside the oven. Transfer the bacon strips and the chickpea egg to the baking sheet to keep warm.

9. Prep the asparagus by breaking off and discarding the tough, woody stems. In a medium pot or large saucepan over medium-high heat, bring 3 cups of water and the salt to a boil. In a medium bowl near the stove, prepare an ice water

This version calls for asparagus, but feel free to move with the seasons and substitute other vegetables, such as sautéed mushrooms or roasted butternut squash. Heating your oven on the lowest setting to keep your ingredients hot until you're ready to plate is a trick I use when I don't have the luxury of multiple line cooks helping me bring this dish together.

bath. Blanch the asparagus for 3 minutes, then plunge the spears into the ice bath for a few minutes, until completely cooled. Drain and dry the spears with a paper towel or clean dish towel and set aside.

10. Heat 2 teaspoons of the oil in a large skillet over medium heat. Add the asparagus spears plus a sprinkle of salt and sauté for 5 to 7 minutes, until the asparagus is tender but not completely soft. (If you have a stovetop grill, you can use that instead and finish the asparagus with some beautiful grill marks.) Transfer the sautéed asparagus to the warm oven.

11. In the same pan over medium heat, add the remaining 2 teaspoons of olive oil and quickly toss the baby spinach with a sprinkle of salt until it is just wilted, 1 to 2 minutes. Transfer the wilted spinach to the oven.

12. Toast the English muffin halves or bread.

13. In a small pot over medium-low heat, gently warm the hollandaise sauce, stirring frequently. If you've made the hollandaise ahead of time, warm for about 10 minutes. If you've just made it, it should only need about 5. Unlike a traditional hollandaise, this one should be warmed just before serving, as it can reduce quickly and become too dense. Taste as you stir to check the consistency. When ready, the hollandaise should be velvety, but not dense or heavy.

14. Remove the baking sheet from the oven. Using the toasted English muffins as your base, layer the following on each muffin half, from the bottom up: 2 tablespoons of barbecue sauce, 2 tempeh bacon strips, 2 tablespoons of sautéed spinach, ¼ cup chickpea egg, another 2 tablespoons of sautéed spinach, and 4 asparagus spears. These quantities are just guidance. You can use your judgment as to how the ingredients will best fit your muffin.

15. Pour a generous portion of the warm hollandaise sauce over each muffin and garnish with a sprinkle of the gremolata or parsley and a twist of black pepper. Serve with the roasted potatoes or simple green salad.

I AM POWERFUL
Crispy Quinoa Cashew Granola

I was inspired to create a superfood granola when Tucker Garrison, co-founder of Imlak'esh Organics, brought me some macambo beans to try. Tucker is based in the Santa Barbara area and specializes in locating ethically sourced superfoods from small-scale organic farmers around the world. The macambo is wild-harvested by a women's collective in the Peruvian Amazon, and it has a lovely, buttery crunch. So it was hard *not* to be moved to use them! Macambo is a part of the same plant family as the cacao bean and has been used for centuries by Amazonian healers to treat brain disorders. It also has a very high protein content and is rich in both fiber and omega-9 fatty acids. You can order this amazing "brain bean" online directly from Imlak'esh, though if you absolutely can't source the macambo, you may replace it with an extra cup of cashews.

I take a lot of pride in this recipe because the granola is so good it's almost like candy—even though it's composed entirely of superfoods such as golden berries, puffed quinoa, cacao, and maca, as well as coconut nectar, which is one of the lowest glycemic sweeteners. At the cafés, we also package I Am Powerful as a parfait in Mason jars for our retail area. Our guests love this offering because it is so pretty and convenient, and you can easily re-create this for yourself by simply layering the granola with a fruit salad and Coconut Yogurt (page 33) and storing a morning-time (or anytime) treat in the refrigerator.

MAKES ABOUT 8 CUPS

2 cups raw cashews, whole or pieces

1 cup macambo beans

½ cup raw macadamia nuts

½ cup dried golden berries

3 cups puffed quinoa (sometimes called quinoa pop or quinoa puffs)

1 cup coconut nectar

1. Preheat the oven to 250°F.

2. Chop the cashews, macambo beans, macadamia nuts, and golden berries into a crumble with pieces no larger than ¼ inch.

3. Transfer the mixture to a large bowl and add the quinoa, coconut nectar, cacao nibs, orange zest, maca, salt, cinnamon, and vanilla. Mix with a spatula or wooden spoon until everything is evenly distributed. The mixture will be sticky and delicious.

recipe and ingredients continue

½ cup raw cacao nibs

Zest of 2 medium oranges

2 teaspoons maca powder

2 teaspoons Himalayan sea salt

½ teaspoon ground cinnamon

¼ teaspoon vanilla extract

4. Spread the granola mixture evenly over 2 large baking sheets. Bake the granola for 40 to 60 minutes, checking it after 20 minutes to turn it over and break up any large chunks. The granola is ready when it is a dark golden color and has dried out slightly.

5. Place the baking sheets on racks to cool, breaking up any large masses of granola, as it will firm up as it cools. When it is completely cool, store the granola in an airtight container or jar for up to 6 weeks.

QUESTION
of the day

Who has made a big difference in your life?

I AM THRILLED
Sourdough French Toast with Cashew Crème Fraiche, Mixed Berries, and Strawberry-Raspberry Reduction

It's hard to do a classic brunch without offering a great French toast. Many people think you need eggs to make this dish, but what I've learned is that you can use any kind of liquid to get the same effect. I created a banana-chia milk, which gets its subtle sweetness from a little maple syrup and has thick enough body to give the toast a nice sumptuous quality. And because I love sweet breakfasts, I wanted to pair the French toast with a strawberry-raspberry reduction and Cashew Crème Fraiche, making it—to my mind—the perfect dish.

We work with a local bread supplier who uses almost entirely heirloom California wheat grains, and the beautiful quality and sour flavor of the bread is part of what makes this French toast really special. I'm a huge fan of sourdough breads in particular, because I believe that they digest better and they have a better taste. If you'd prefer to use a yeasted or vegan brioche-style bread for this, that's okay, too. I also enjoy this made with a baguette, including a gluten-free version. And if preparing this for kids, I recommend slicing the bread into dipping-friendly fingers.

SERVES 4

For the Banana-Chia Milk:
1 cup Coconut Milk (page 32) or store-bought

½ cup coconut sugar

½ cup mashed ripe banana

1 tablespoon chia seeds

1 teaspoon maple syrup

½ teaspoon vanilla extract

1. Make the banana-chia milk: In a blender, combine the coconut milk, coconut sugar, banana, chia seeds, maple syrup, and vanilla and blend until creamy. Pour into a shallow dish or bowl and set aside.

2. Make the strawberry-raspberry reduction: Rinse the strawberries under cold water and transfer them to a food processor. (No need to stem them since you will be straining the pulp before cooking.) Add the raspberries as well and process just until the berries are reduced to a liquid. Do not overprocess, as that will make it more difficult to strain.

recipe and ingredients continue

For the Strawberry-Raspberry
Reduction:

1 pound fresh strawberries

1 pound fresh raspberries

¼ cup cane sugar

2 teaspoons fresh lemon juice

To Assemble:

Coconut oil, for the pan

Eight 1-inch-thick slices fresh
or day-old sourdough bread

Cashew Crème Fraiche
(page 315)

Fresh mixed berries of
your choice

Maple syrup, for drizzling

3. Over a medium saucepan, pass the berry mixture through a fine-mesh sieve to remove all the seeds, stems, and excess fiber of the fruit. Stir in the sugar and lemon juice.

4. Bring the berry mixture to a boil over medium heat and continue to cook, stirring frequently, until the fruit has stopped foaming, about 7 minutes. Skim off any foam that forms on the surface of the sauce. Reduce the heat enough to keep the sauce at a low boil and continue cooking until the sauce thickens and coats the back of your spoon, 5 to 7 minutes. Remove the pan from the heat and set aside to cool.

5. Assemble: Heat a large, heavy-bottomed skillet over medium heat. (I love a well-seasoned cast-iron skillet for French toast and pancakes, but a nonstick pan also works very well.) Add 1 tablespoon of the coconut oil to heat.

6. Soak slices of the sourdough bread quickly—10 to 15 seconds—in the banana-chia milk. You don't want them to soak too long or they will become soggy. Add the bread to the pan and cook for about 5 minutes on each side, or until a nice crust has formed. Transfer the finished French toast to a plate or, better yet, a low oven to keep it nice and hot. Work in batches until all of the bread is finished, adding a dab of coconut oil as needed to prevent sticking.

7. Finish the French toast with a generous dollop of cashew crème fraiche, a drizzle of the strawberry-raspberry sauce, fresh mixed berries, and maple syrup.

I AM HOLY
Baked Gluten-Free Donuts

These have become a highlight of our bakery case repertoire. They're baked donuts, versus fried, and we have a lot of fun decorating them with all manner of glazes. Here I've given you the base recipe for the donuts and our three most popular glaze variations: white coconut, chocolate, and strawberry. You can also get creative with sprinklings on top—coconut flakes, nuts, fresh or dried fruit. Let your inspiration be your guide.

MAKES 12 DONUTS

For the Batter:

¼ cup ground golden flaxseeds

¼ cup coconut oil, melted and slightly cooled, plus more for the pan

1½ cups Gluten-Free All-Purpose Bakery Flour Blend (page 34) or store-bought

¾ cup coconut sugar

¼ teaspoon Himalayan sea salt

1½ cups Coconut Milk (page 32) or store-bought

⅛ teaspoon vanilla extract

For Decorating:

1 batch of Glaze (recipes follow)

Coconut flakes, for sprinkling (optional)

Chopped nuts, for sprinkling (optional)

Chopped fresh or dried fruit, for sprinkling (optional)

1. Make the batter: In a medium bowl, whisk together the ground flaxseeds with ½ cup of warm water and allow to sit for 10 minutes.

2. Preheat the oven to 325°F. Grease a 12-mold donut tray with coconut oil or cooking spray and set aside.

3. In a large bowl, combine the flour, coconut sugar, and salt.

4. Once the flax mixture has thickened, add the coconut milk, coconut oil, and vanilla to the bowl and whisk to combine. Stir this mixture into the dry ingredients and mix until just combined, being careful not to overmix.

5. If you have a pastry bag with a wide round tip, you can transfer the batter to the pastry bag and use it to pipe the batter into the donut molds. If not, you can use a spoon to fill each mold about three-quarters full of batter, making sure it is evenly distributed.

6. Bake the donuts for 12 minutes, until golden. Allow them to cool completely in the pan before decorating them. You can make the glazes while the donuts cool.

7. Using a small spatula, glaze the donuts and decorate them as you like.

recipe and ingredients continue

White Coconut Glaze:

½ cup powdered sugar

1 tablespoon Coconut Milk (page 32) or store-bought

In a small bowl, whisk together the powdered sugar and coconut milk. It will come together as a thicker glaze, but you can add 1 to 2 more teaspoons of coconut milk for a runnier glaze.

Chocolate Glaze:

½ cup powdered sugar

¼ cup raw cacao powder

1½ tablespoons Coconut Milk (page 32) or store-bought

In a small bowl, whisk together the powdered sugar, cacao powder, and coconut milk. It will come together as a thicker glaze, but you can add 1 to 2 more teaspoons of coconut milk for a runnier glaze.

Strawberry Glaze:

½ cup powdered sugar

2 small ripe and juicy fresh strawberries, hulled

In a medium bowl, add the powdered sugar and smash in the strawberries using a fork or spoon. The strawberries will give the glaze its color as they release their juices, which also serve as the liquid. The strawberries need to be ripe and juicy in order for this to work! If you have only larger strawberries, simply add more powdered sugar until you reach the desired consistency.

NOTE Nowadays it's easy to find donut trays at most large retailers or online. Our donuts are approximately 4 inches in diameter. You are welcome to use a tray with different dimensions, though you will need to play with the baking time.

I AM OPEN-HEARTED
Gluten-Free Buckwheat Flax Pancakes with Seasonal Fruit and Cashew Coconut Butter

These buckwheat-based pancakes are hands-down the top-selling breakfast item at Café Gratitude. They are rustic and hearty without being heavy, and with the seasonal fruit, whipped cashew coconut butter (see Note), and a drizzle of maple syrup, they're truly delicious. In addition to being gluten-free, these pancakes are also grain-free, as buckwheat, despite its name and appearance, is a relative of the rhubarb and sorrel family.

SERVES 4

For the Cashew Coconut Butter:

½ cup raw cashews

2 tablespoons cane sugar

Pinch of Himalayan sea salt

⅓ cup coconut oil

For the Pancakes:

1½ cups Almond Milk (page 30) or store-bought

1 teaspoon apple cider vinegar

1 tablespoon ground flaxseeds

1 cup buckwheat flour

1 tablespoon coconut sugar

1 teaspoon baking powder

1 teaspoon baking soda

⅛ teaspoon Himalayan sea salt

¼ teaspoon vanilla extract

Coconut oil, for the pan

1. Make the cashew coconut butter: In a blender, combine the cashews, cane sugar, salt, and ¾ cup of water. Blend until the mixture becomes a smooth cream. Add the coconut oil and continue blending until the mixture is completely smooth and uniform. Pour the butter into a covered container and let it set up in the refrigerator for 8 to 12 hours.

2. Make the pancakes: In a small bowl, whisk together the almond milk and apple cider vinegar and set aside to sour for 10 minutes. The almond "buttermilk" adds a nice tang to the pancakes and the acid in the apple cider vinegar also works as a leavening agent with the baking soda to give extra fluffiness to the pancakes.

3. In another small bowl, whisk together the ground flaxseeds and 3 tablespoons of warm water. Allow the mixture to sit for 10 minutes, or until the mixture is gelatinous.

4. In a large bowl, mix together the buckwheat flour, coconut sugar, baking powder, baking soda, and salt. Whisk in the almond buttermilk and the flax mixture until combined. Add the vanilla.

recipe and ingredients continue

For Serving:

Seasonal fresh fruit

Maple syrup (I like dark amber, sometimes called "Grade B," though it has nothing to do with the quality, just when in the season the syrup is harvested)

Powdered sugar

5. In a large skillet over medium heat, heat about a tablespoon of the coconut oil. When the pan is warm, spoon the batter into the pan, using about ¼ cup batter for each pancake, and allow to cook for 2 to 3 minutes, until there are bubbles on the surface and the edges have set. Flip the pancakes and cook 1 to 2 minutes longer and set the finished pancakes on a platter. Keep covered under a clean towel. Repeat with the remaining batter.

6. Serve the warm pancakes with an abundant scoop of seasonal fruit, a generous dab of the cashew coconut butter, and the maple syrup, and finish with a sprinkle of powdered sugar.

NOTE If you choose to make the cashew coconut butter, you will need to start it a day in advance so that it has time to set up. You can also make a soft cashew coconut whipped cream instead by reducing the coconut oil to ¼ cup and letting it set up in the refrigerator.

QUESTION *of the day* / For whom do you make a difference?

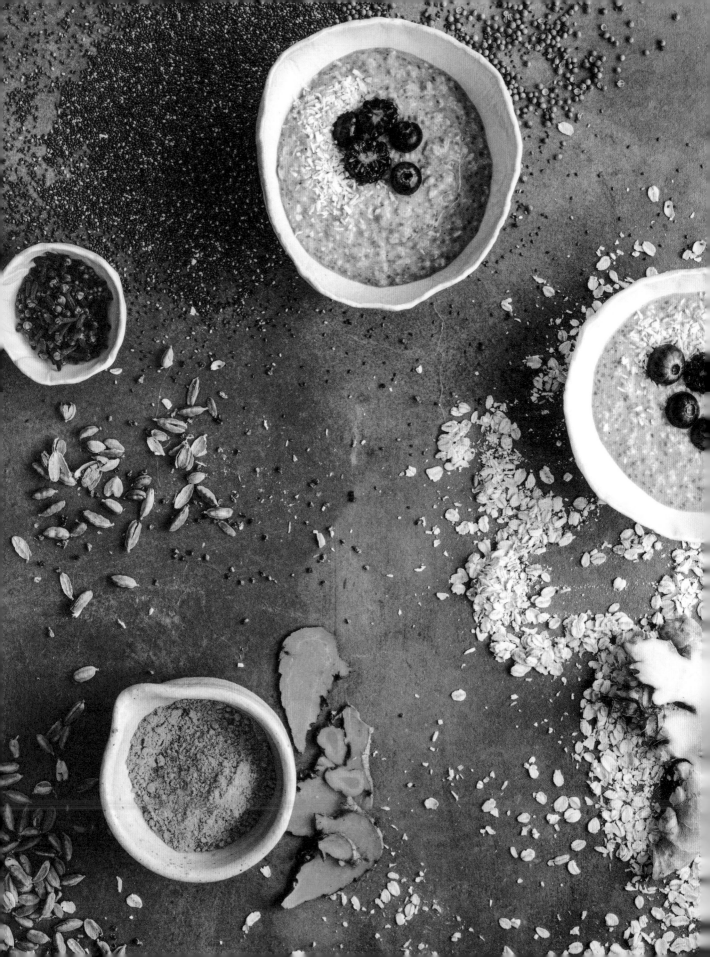

I AM PATIENT
Turmeric Chia Overnight Oats

When I came up with this dish, I was going for the kind of breakfast that you could eat every day—something that wouldn't be too heavy, too involved, or too cumbersome to have on the go. I was particularly looking toward using ingredients that would be beneficial before or after a workout. That brought me to anti-inflammatory turmeric and ginger, protein-rich chia seeds, and oats, which are not only a great source of iron and protein but are also just generally healthy and delightfully substantial. The preparation couldn't be easier—it's just a bunch of ingredients mixed together and stored in the refrigerator, so you can make a batch and be set for the week. You can also make any adjustments to your preferences, whether it's adding a pinch of cardamom or a handful of nuts, seeds, or dried fruits that you enjoy.

SERVES 4

For the Almond-Date Milk:

2¼ cups Almond Milk (page 30) or store-bought

3 Medjool dates, pitted

For the Overnight Oats:

2 cups rolled oats

2 tablespoons chia seeds

2 tablespoons fresh turmeric juice or 2 teaspoons dried ground turmeric mixed with 2 tablespoons of water

2 tablespoons fresh ginger juice or 2 teaspoons dried ground ginger mixed with 2 tablespoons of water

¼ teaspoon vanilla extract

¼ teaspoon ground cinnamon

For Serving:

Fresh blueberries

Shredded coconut

Hempseeds

1. Make the almond-date milk: In a blender, combine the almond milk and dates and blend until the dates are completely dissolved. (If you don't have a high-speed blender, or if your dates seem a bit dry, you can soak the dates in warm water for at least 30 minutes to soften them prior to blending.)

2. Make the overnight oats: In a large bowl, combine the almond-date milk, rolled oats, chia seeds, turmeric juice, ginger juice, vanilla, and cinnamon. Mix well, cover, and chill for at least 8 hours. It's nice to set this up before you go to bed so it's ready in the morning.

3. Check the consistency of the oats and adjust for your personal taste. You can thin them out with a bit of almond milk or water to reach your desired consistency.

4. Serve: Divide the overnight oats among 4 bowls or jars and garnish with blueberries, shredded coconut, and hempseeds.

I AM BRIGHT-EYED
Raw Apple Pecan Porridge with Coconut Milk and Strawberries

This fresh, easy-to-prepare raw porridge was a staple on early Café Gratitude menus and is still a favorite that makes guest appearances in the fall. Everything gets pulsed in the blender together until just before it becomes a smoothie—though you could go that route, too!

SERVES 2

For the Porridge:

1 large apple (preferably Honeycrisp or Fuji), cored and roughly chopped

5 large ripe fresh strawberries, hulled, or other seasonal berries

1½ cups Coconut Milk (page 32) or store-bought

½ cup raw pecans

½ teaspoon vanilla extract

Big pinch of ground cinnamon

Pinch of Himalayan sea salt

For Serving:

4 fresh strawberries, hulled and sliced

6 raw pecans, chopped

Ground cinnamon, for sprinkling

1. Make the porridge: In a blender, combine the apple, strawberries, coconut milk, pecans, vanilla, cinnamon, and salt. Pulse until you have reached your desired consistency, chunky or smooth.

2. Transfer the porridge to serving bowls and garnish with sliced strawberries, chopped pecans, and a sprinkle of cinnamon.

I AM SERENE
Gluten-Free Cinnamon Rolls

To me these are the apex of our accomplishments as an organic, gluten-free, vegan bakery. They have all the softness, density, and gooey, chewy deliciousness of a traditional cinnamon roll and are every bit as worthy of the effort to make them. I highly recommend making an extra batch, freezing the unbaked rolls, and baking them from frozen whenever the mood strikes. (Just add 3 to 5 minutes to the baking time.) And while we serve ours with a powdered sugar glaze, feel free to skip this and simply sprinkle the rolls with more of the cinnamon filling.

MAKES 6 ROLLS

For the Cinnamon Filling:

1 cup coconut sugar

2 tablespoons ground cinnamon

1 tablespoon coconut oil

1 tablespoon maple syrup

¼ teaspoon Himalayan sea salt

For the Dough:

1½ cups Gluten-Free All-Purpose Bakery Flour Blend (page 34), plus more for rolling out the dough

2 tablespoons plus 1 teaspoon baking powder

2 tablespoons psyllium husk powder

1 tablespoon coconut sugar

½ teaspoon baking soda

¼ teaspoon Himalayan sea salt

1½ cups Coconut Milk (page 32) or store-bought

3 tablespoons coconut oil, melted and slightly cooled

1. Make the cinnamon filling: In a medium bowl, combine the coconut sugar, cinnamon, coconut oil, maple syrup, and salt and mix well. The mixture will be dense and crumbly. Set aside.

2. Make the dough: Line a baking sheet with parchment paper or a silicone baking mat and set aside.

3. In a large bowl, sift together the flour blend, baking powder, psyllium powder, coconut sugar, baking soda, and salt.

4. In a medium bowl, whisk together the coconut milk, coconut oil, lemon juice, apple cider vinegar, and vanilla.

5. Add the wet ingredient mixture to the sifted dry ingredients and mix to combine. The dough will be quite dense, so at some point you'll want to start using your hands and begin kneading. Continue working the dough until it is smooth, 2 to 3 minutes.

6. Preheat the oven to 325°F.

7. Lightly dust a board or clean surface with the flour blend. Transfer the dough to the prepared work surface.

recipe and ingredients continue

1 tablespoon fresh lemon juice

1 tablespoon apple cider vinegar

½ teaspoon vanilla extract

2 tablespoons fresh orange juice

For the Glaze:

½ cup powdered sugar

1 tablespoon Coconut Milk (page 32) or store-bought, plus more if needed

8. Using your hands, gently stretch and form the dough into a rectangular shape. Use a rolling pin to roll out the dough until it is roughly 12 inches by 4 inches and approximately ½ inch thick.

9. Spread the cinnamon filling over the dough in a thin, even layer, pressing it lightly into the dough.

10. Roll the dough up the long side into a long tube shape, rolling tightly to prevent the cinnamon filling from escaping. You should be able to roll the dough 2 full rotations.

11. Cut the tube into 6 rolls, each about 2 inches thick. Place each roll, swirl-side up, onto the prepared baking sheet. Take this opportunity to gently pat the rolls down so they're flat on top, and adjust them, if needed, to make sure they are nice and tight.

12. Using a pastry brush, brush each roll with the orange juice. This will give the rolls a nice golden tone when they're baked, much like a traditional egg wash.

13. Bake for 20 minutes. Check the rolls at 15 minutes to see how they are doing; they should be golden but still soft to the touch when they come out of the oven.

14. Allow the rolls to cool completely in the pan.

15. Make the glaze: In a small bowl, whisk together the powdered sugar and the coconut milk. This will create a rather thick glaze. For a thinner glaze, you can add 1 or 2 more teaspoons of coconut milk. Drizzle over the cinnamon rolls.

I AM BEAUTIFUL
Gluten-Free Muffins

When we first started offering baked goods at Café Gratitude, I tried putting out whole-wheat or Kamut flour muffins, but for some reason we couldn't sell them. Then I turned to the gluten-free pantry, and these muffins have since become a must-have in our case. They are easy to prepare, are a great way to use seasonal fruit, and are really, truly muffins—not cupcakes parading as such. Because over the years we've found that not all fruit works equally well, I've included three of our favorite combinations: Strawberry–, Raspberry–, or Banana–Chocolate Chip; Peach-Blueberry; and Lemon–Poppy seed.

MAKES 24 MUFFINS

1 cup coconut oil, melted and slightly cooled, plus more for the pan(s)

2 tablespoons ground golden flaxseeds

4 cups Gluten-Free All-Purpose Bakery Flour Blend (page 34)

¾ cup coconut sugar, plus more for sprinkling

½ teaspoon Himalayan sea salt

2¾ cups Coconut Milk (page 32) or store-bought

¼ teaspoon vanilla extract

FLAVOR VARIATIONS

Strawberry–, Raspberry–, or Banana–Chocolate Chip

3 cups sliced fresh strawberries, raspberries, or ripe banana

1 cup vegan chocolate chips

Peach-Blueberry

3 cups cubed, peeled peaches

1 cup blueberries

1. Make the muffin batter: Preheat the oven to 325°F. Coat two 12-cup muffin pans with coconut oil or cooking spray. Set aside.

2. In a small bowl, whisk the ground flaxseeds with ½ cup of warm water and set aside for 10 minutes to gel.

3. For lemon-poppy seed, we like to completely blend the coconut milk with the whole lemon, peel and all. It gives the muffins an amazing zesty and rich lemon flavor.

4. In a medium bowl, combine the flour blend, coconut sugar, and salt. Add the coconut milk, vanilla, flaxseed mixture, and, depending on what variation you've chosen, the fruit/chocolate/poppy seeds. Mix until the ingredients are just combined. With the strawberry, raspberry, and peach-blueberry variations you can squeeze some of the fruit using your hands—you will see how it lends a nice color to the batter.

5. For the banana-chocolate, you'll want to mash most of the bananas, leaving about a quarter of them in large chunks.

recipe and ingredients continue

Lemon–Poppy Seed

3 tablespoons poppy seeds

1 whole lemon, halved and seeds removed

For the Glaze:

½ cup powdered sugar (optional)

1 tablespoon fresh lemon juice (optional), plus more if needed

6. Once you've added the variation ingredients, stir in the 1 cup coconut oil. This will thicken the batter, help it to set up, and make it easier to scoop. Spoon ¼ cup of batter into each muffin cup and sprinkle a good amount of coconut sugar over the top of each.

7. You also have the option of making a glaze: In a small bowl, whisk together the powdered sugar and lemon juice until smooth. The glaze will be thick, so you can add another teaspoon or 2 of lemon juice for a runnier glaze.

8. Bake for 25 to 30 minutes, until the muffins are golden brown, and a toothpick or tester inserted into the middle of a muffin comes out without crumbs. Cool in the pan for 5 minutes, then transfer the muffins to a cooling rack. Drizzle with the glaze, if using, while the muffins are still warm.

APPETIZERS
& SNACKS

Rosemary, Butternut Squash,
and Radicchio
(page 89)

Broccolini with
Macadamia Cheddar
(page 90)

Warm Artichoke
and Spinach Dip
(opposite)

I AM COMMUNITY

This appetizer truly earns its affirmation namesake by being one of the most popular appetizers that guests love to share. We use the same creamy base and add seasonal considerations. Since we really only have two seasons in Southern California, we offer the classic Artichoke and Spinach version during the spring/summer; Rosemary, Butternut Squash, and Radicchio for fall/winter; and then Broccolini with Macadamia Cheddar as an option to make all year-round. You can also use this standard process and feel free to experiment with your favorite vegetable combos.

Warm Artichoke and Spinach Dip

SERVES 4

2 cups artichoke hearts (from fresh baby artichokes; jarred; or frozen and thawed)

Juice of two lemons, if using fresh artichokes

3 tablespoons extra-virgin olive oil

1 garlic clove, smashed

2 tablespoons capers in brine, drained and chopped

½ teaspoon Himalayan sea salt

¼ cup white wine

1 recipe Cashew Cream (page 311)

2 cups packed baby spinach, roughly chopped

Assorted crostini, crackers, or vegetable crudité for dipping

The original reference for this seasonally rotating trio of dips was the classic warm spinach-artichoke dip, which is usually pretty heavy with cream and cheeses. Our version is considerably lightened with cashew cream but it's just as dangerously good.

1. Fill a large bowl with 4 cups of cold water and add the lemon juice. Using a serrated knife, cut off the top third of one of the artichokes and discard the leaves, as they will be too tough to use. Begin to pull back the outer leaves, allowing them to snap off at the base until you have reached the tender green inner leaves and can no longer easily remove the leaves.

2. If you have some stem to work with, cut ¼ inch off the bottom and use a vegetable peeler to remove the tough outer skin.

3. Use a paring knife to trim away any rough bits where you snapped off the leaves and then cut the artichoke in half. If there is a hairy choke that looks overgrown, remove it.

4. Repeat with the remaining artichokes, dropping the prepped artichokes into the lemon-water bath as you go, to

recipe continues

keep them from turning black. Keep them in the lemon water until you are ready to sauté them; you may store them in the lemon water for up to 2 days in the refrigerator.

5. Drain the artichoke hearts. In a large, heavy-bottomed sauté pan over medium heat, warm the olive oil for 1 minute, then add the smashed garlic clove. Allow it to brown for 2 minutes, reducing the heat if it looks like it's browning too fast. Add the capers to the pan and allow them to lightly fry for about 30 seconds. Add the artichoke hearts to the pan and turn them in the pan until they're well coated with the caper-infused olive oil. Sprinkle the artichokes with the salt and partially cover the skillet. Sauté the artichokes for 7 to 10 minutes, until somewhat softened, turning them when necessary to keep them from burning. If the pan gets very dry, you may add a few tablespoons of water as needed.

6. Add the white wine and deglaze the pan, loosening any small, delicious bits that may be stuck to the bottom of the pan. Remove the pan from the heat, cover the pan, and allow the artichokes to sit for 5 minutes. They are ready when they are soft and are beginning to break apart. Discard the garlic clove.

7. Preheat the oven to 400°F.

8. In a large bowl, combine the cashew cream and the artichoke mixture. Give everything a toss, add the spinach, and toss once more. Add half of the mixture to a food processor and pulse until the mixture is thick yet still chunky. Return the blended mix to the bowl and combine with the unprocessed artichoke-spinach mixture.

9. Transfer the mixture to a small baking dish (such as a 9-inch x 9-inch square or a 6-inch round) and bake for 20 to 30 minutes, until the dip has puffed up slightly and has a golden-brown surface. Let the dip sit for 5 minutes before serving. It's best served warm but can also be served at room temperature with a selection of crostini, crackers, or vegetable crudité.

To make these seasonal variations, prepare your cashew cream base according to the recipe and follow the same procedure as the Warm Artichoke and Spinach Dip, changing out the artichoke sauté for the sautéed vegetables described below.

Rosemary, Butternut Squash, and Radicchio

SERVES 4

3 tablespoons extra-virgin olive oil

¼ cup finely chopped red onion

1 small butternut squash, peeled, seeded, and diced

2 teaspoons finely chopped fresh rosemary

¼ teaspoon smoked salt or Himalayan sea salt

¼ cup white wine

1 recipe Cashew Cream (page 311)

½ small head of red radicchio, shredded

A rich, lucious dip for the fall or winter.

1. Heat the olive oil in a large, heavy-bottomed skillet over medium heat. Add the onion and cook until the onion becomes translucent, about 1 minute. Add the squash, rosemary, and salt and stir well. Partially cover the skillet and cook until the squash has softened a bit, 5 to 7 minutes, adding a few tablespoons of water if the pan begins to look dry. Add the white wine and deglaze the pan, loosening any small, delicious bits that may be stuck to the bottom of the pan.

2. When the wine has been absorbed, remove the pan from the heat, cover, and let it sit for 5 minutes. The butternut squash is ready when it is soft and beginning to break apart.

3. In a large bowl, combine the cashew cream, butternut squash mixture, and radicchio. Process half of the mixture in a food processor, mix that back into the remaining mixture, and bake following the same instructions on page 86.

Broccolini with Macadamia Cheddar

SERVES 3

3 tablespoons extra-virgin olive oil

1 garlic clove, smashed

¼ cup finely chopped red onion

2 to 3 bunches broccolini, stems chopped and florets left whole (about 4 cups)

¼ teaspoon smoked salt or Himalayan sea salt

⅛ teaspoon red chili flakes (optional)

¼ cup white wine

1 recipe Cashew Cream (page 311)

1 heaping tablespoon Macadamia Cheddar (page 316)

Minced chives, for garnish (optional)

The perfect indulgent year-round appetizer.

1. Heat the olive oil in a large, heavy-bottomed skillet over medium heat. Add the garlic and onion and cook until the onion becomes translucent, about 1 minute.

2. Stir in the broccolini, salt, and red chili flakes, if using. Partially cover the skillet and allow the broccolini to cook until it softens and is brightly colored, 5 to 7 minutes, adding a few tablespoons of water if the pan gets too dry.

3. Add the white wine and deglaze the pan, loosening any small, delicious bits that may be stuck to the bottom. When the wine has been absorbed, remove the pan from the heat, cover, and let it sit for 5 minutes. Discard the garlic clove.

4. In a large bowl, combine the broccolini mixture and the cashew cream. Process half of the mixture in a food processor, mix that back into the remaining mixture, and transfer the dip to a shallow baking dish. Distribute dabs of the macadamia cheddar on top of the broccolini mixture and bake according to the instructions on page 86. Garnish with chives, if desired.

I AM ABUNDANT

Italian Antipasto Plate with Herbed Cashew Mozzarella, Bistro Pickled Carrots, Eggplant Caponata, Oven-Roasted Yellow Peppers and Olives, and Fennel Salad with Gremolata and Smoked Salt

This colorful, flavor-packed antipasto plate is a standout on our summer menus, showcasing vibrant summer produce with Mediterranean flair. Using our versatile cashew mozzarella cheese as the centerpiece, you can mix and match these dishes on your antipasto platter as you wish. Make each of them, or simply focus on only one or two. The caponata is a lighter, Gratitude-style take on the classic Sicilian summer relish. Tossing the eggplant in a little olive oil and salt and then roasting it in the oven brings out the savory creaminess of the eggplant without the heaviness that frying can sometimes bring. And the natural sweetness of the eggplant and raisins is perfectly balanced and grounded by bittersweet chocolate, a traditional Sicilian addition.

The simple and sublime roasted yellow pepper antipasto was the first dish my Italian mentor Maddalena taught me to make and is one of the many that found their way onto the menu of Café Gratitude over the years. The recipe is very simple and depends entirely on the quality of the yellow bell peppers. In California the only place I have been able to find peppers as flavorful as the sweet yellow ones I became accustomed to in Italy has been at our local farmers markets in late summer.

And the fennel salad provides a welcome crunchiness while cleansing the palate. You can shave the fennel so that it is more of a garnish or cut it into small wedges like a crudité.

However you choose to assemble your platter, remember that grilled sourdough baguette slices are a must, and don't forget to dress up the plate with some pickles (especially our Bistro Pickled Carrots [page 323]), fresh vegetable crudité (especially heirloom cherry tomatoes), olives, and lightly toasted almonds. All of these dishes can be made a day or two in advance and will, in fact, benefit flavorwise from the extra time.

recipe and ingredients continue

For the Eggplant Caponata:

3 large eggplants, cut into 1-inch cubes

½ cup extra-virgin olive oil, plus more if needed

1¼ teaspoons Himalayan sea salt, plus more to taste

½ cup finely chopped red onion

1 celery stalk, sliced into slim half-moons (about ½ cup)

¼ teaspoon freshly ground black pepper

1 tablespoon Compassionate Blend (page 26) (optional)

2 tablespoons raisins (we use Thompson), soaked for 30 minutes in warm water to cover, then drained

½ cup finely diced Roma tomatoes

2 tablespoons roughly chopped green olives (any pitted green variety will work)

3 ounces bittersweet baking chocolate, finely chopped

2 teaspoons capers, in brine, drained

⅓ cup apple cider vinegar

¼ cup coconut sugar

Fresh basil leaves, for garnish

1 tablespoon pine nuts, for garnish (optional)

For the Oven-Roasted Yellow Peppers and Olives:

2 pounds (about 8) yellow bell peppers, cored, seeded, and cut into 2-inch chunks

1 cup pitted green olives (any type is fine)

¼ cup capers in brine, drained

1. Make the eggplant caponata: Preheat the oven to 375°F.

2. In a large bowl, toss the eggplants with ¼ cup of the olive oil and 1 teaspoon of the salt. Transfer the eggplants to a baking sheet and bake for 15 minutes, then stir the eggplants. Continue to check every 5 minutes until soft and translucent, for a total of 25 to 30 minutes. Transfer the eggplants to a mixing bowl and set aside to cool while you make the marinade.

3. In a large, heavy-bottomed skillet or wide, flat saucepan over medium heat, heat the remaining ¼ cup of olive oil for 1 minute. Add the onion, celery, remaining ¼ teaspoon of salt, and the pepper. Cook for 2 minutes, until the onion becomes translucent.

4. If you are using the compassionate blend, add it now, otherwise you may add an additional tablespoon of olive oil if the sauté seems dry. Continue to cook for an additional minute or 2 until the compassionate blend has melted and infused into the onion mixture. Add the soaked raisins, tomatoes, green olives, chocolate, and capers. Allow the marinade to cook down for an additional 10 minutes, until it begins to thicken.

5. Add the apple cider vinegar and coconut sugar and cook for 2 to 3 minutes, until the acid of the vinegar has cooked off. Pour the warm marinade over the eggplants, mix well, and adjust for salt to taste. Allow the mixture to marinate for an hour or more before serving. Garnish with the basil and pine nuts, if using.

6. Make the oven-roasted yellow peppers and olives: Preheat the oven to 350°F.

7. In a large bowl, combine the peppers, olives, capers, and garlic. Drizzle the olive oil evenly over the mixture and toss to evenly coat the peppers. Sprinkle the breadcrumbs, salt, and black pepper over the mixture and toss once more until just combined.

recipe and ingredients continue

2 garlic cloves, smashed and chopped

½ cup extra-virgin olive oil

¼ cup finely ground breadcrumbs

1 teaspoon Himalayan sea salt

1 teaspoon freshly ground black pepper

To Assemble:

2 medium fennel bulbs, outer layers removed, sliced very thin (a mandoline is perfect here), or cut into small wedges

Extra-virgin olive oil, to taste

Smoked salt, to taste

Gremolata (page 293), to taste

Herbed Cashew Mozzarella (page 313)

Bistro Pickled Carrots (page 323)

Toasted almonds (optional)

Heirloom cherry tomatoes or other seasonal vegetables (optional)

Grilled or toasted baguette slices or crackers

8. Turn the mixture out onto a large baking sheet and bake for 40 to 45 minutes, until the peppers are very soft but still hold their shape. After the first 20 minutes, you will want to check them every so often and turn them over in the pan. Don't be afraid to really cook the peppers until they are creamy. Remember that you're going to be scooping them onto crispy crostini! This dish can be eaten warm, at room temperature, or even lightly chilled.

9. To assemble: In a medium bowl, toss the fennel with a drizzle of olive oil, a sprinkle of smoked salt, and a small dollop of gremolata.

10. On a large serving platter or perhaps a nice wooden cutting board, assemble the herbed cashew mozzarella, eggplant caponata, roasted yellow peppers, and bistro pickled carrots. Garnish the plate with the fennel salad and dress it up with some toasted almonds, if desired, and maybe a few heirloom cherry tomatoes or other seasonal vegetables of your choice. Serve with the sourdough crostini or your favorite bread or crackers.

I AM BRIGHT
Sautéed Broccolini with Tempeh Bacon and Avocado Cream

I love broccolini, and I wanted to dress it up a bit more than the usual garlic–and–chili-flake sauté. I was looking through recipes for inspiration and came across a really beautiful avocado and cream combination with fennel that sounded so unique and fresh. I gave it the Gratitude treatment by using coconut yogurt, imparting it with a bright tanginess that works so nicely with the tempeh bacon. All the components together make for a light, summery, smoky, vegetable-forward appetizer plate that can also do double duty as a side dish served with an entrée or at a potluck or barbecue.

I call for sautéing the broccolini in a skillet here, but cooking it on a stovetop grill or a barbecue is a great alternative. In that case, you would toss the blanched broccolini in the olive oil, garlic, smoked salt, and red chili flakes first and then toss them on the hot grill, which has the advantage of giving you some nice grill marks and even smokier flavor. And if you are fortunate enough to come across some broccoli rabe, also known as rapini, at your local farmers market, it works beautifully in this recipe. Look for bunches that have small leaves and florets that have not yet begun to flower.

SERVES 4

For the Avocado Cream:
1 large or 2 small avocados, diced (about ¾ cup)

½ cup Coconut Yogurt (page 33) or store-bought plain, unsweetened coconut yogurt

¼ cup apple cider vinegar

¼ cup finely chopped fresh fennel, fronds reserved for garnish

2 tablespoons extra-virgin olive oil

¾ teaspoon Himalayan sea salt

1. Make the avocado cream: In a blender, combine the avocado, coconut yogurt, apple cider vinegar, fennel, olive oil, salt, and ¾ cup of water. Blend until smooth and creamy. It should be thick enough to hold its shape when drizzled onto the broccolini. Set aside or refrigerate for up to 3 days.

2. Make the broccolini: Fill a large pot with 4 quarts of water and the sea salt and bring it to a boil over high heat while you prep the broccolini.

3. Trim any thick, woody broccolini stems. When we are serving this dish in the cafés, we like to keep the broccolini stalks whole, but you could cut them into smaller pieces if you like. Just make sure you keep the florets intact.

recipe and ingredients continue

For the Broccolini:

1 tablespoon Himalayan sea salt

4 bunches broccolini

2 tablespoons plus 1 teaspoon
extra-virgin olive oil

1 garlic clove, finely chopped

¼ teaspoon smoked salt,
plus more for serving

⅛ teaspoon red chili flakes,
plus more for serving (optional)

4 slices Tempeh Bacon
(see page 56) or 2 slices of
store-bought

NOTE If you have extra
avocado cream left over,
it makes a great salad
dressing, particularly when
served over late-summer
goodies like cucumber,
watermelon, or tomatoes,
which are really enhanced
by its fresh, fatty embrace.
If you decide to use a
store-bought yogurt for the
avocado cream, make sure
you buy an unflavored or
plain version. Our house
coconut yogurt is lightly
sweetened and that works
well with this recipe, but
better to use caution with a
store-bought version.

4. In a large bowl, prepare an ice bath for the broccolini and
set it near the pot.

5. Carefully add the broccolini to the boiling water and allow
it to return to a boil. Once it boils again, cook the broccolini
for 1 minute and remove it with metal tongs or a strainer
and plunge it into the ice water. Depending on the size of
your pot, feel free to work in batches when blanching the
broccolini. If you blanch in small batches rather than try to
blanch a large amount at once, you will have more control
over the cooking time. Just make sure to bring the water back
to a boil between batches.

6. Transfer the broccolini from the ice water to a colander
to drain.

7. In a large, heavy-bottomed skillet over medium heat,
warm 2 tablespoons of the olive oil for 30 seconds. Add the
chopped garlic and sauté for 30 seconds until it is golden.
Add the blanched, drained broccolini to the pan and toss
it with the garlic oil. Sprinkle with the smoked salt and
chili flakes, if using, and sauté for 2 to 3 minutes, until the
broccolini is heated through yet maintains its bright green
color. You will know the broccolini is ready if the stalks give a
little when you squeeze them between your fingers.

8. Transfer the broccolini to a plate and set aside. Or transfer
the broccolini to a baking pan and keep it in a low oven while
you fry the tempeh bacon.

9. In the same skillet over medium-high heat, heat the
remaining teaspoon of oil. Lightly fry the tempeh bacon for
2 minutes on each side or until it is just crisped.

10. Arrange the broccolini on a (preferably warmed) serving
dish. Crumble the tempeh bacon over the top and drizzle
with the avocado cream. Garnish with a few pinches of red
chili flakes, if desired, and smoked salt. This is a dish best
served warm, but it is also delicious at room temperature if
you keep each of the elements separate just before serving.

I AM BRILLIANT
Young-Coconut Ceviche with Coconut Bacon and Nacho Chips

We have made coconut ceviche at Café Gratitude since our earliest incarnation as a raw food restaurant, and it is a crowd-pleaser that has gone through many different adaptations over the years. This particular recipe is the one I keep coming back to, so I am going to go ahead and call it the definitive Gratitude Coconut Ceviche. It is the perfect dish to make when the weather is warm and green tomatillos are in season, though you could substitute Green Zebra or Roma tomatoes. The coconut bacon adds an unexpected, spicy crunch that is offset by the creaminess of the avocado. In fact once you try this bacon alternative, you'll want to double the recipe so that you can crumble it on almost everything. It's that good.

SERVES 4

For the Ceviche:

2 cups shredded young Thai coconut, frozen and thawed or fresh (see page 32)

1 cup ¼-inch-dice yellow zucchini squash

¼ cup plus 1 tablespoon fresh orange juice

¼ cup fresh lime juice

1 teaspoon Himalayan sea salt

2 teaspoons Compassionate Blend (page 26)

2 teaspoons coconut oil

½ cup diced green tomatillos

2 tablespoons finely chopped red onion

1 teaspoon dulse flakes or granules

⅛ teaspoon red chili flakes

1. Make the ceviche: In a large bowl, combine the coconut, squash, orange juice, lime juice, and salt. Mix well until the salt is dissolved. Cover the bowl and place it in the refrigerator to marinate for at least 8 hours or overnight.

2. Strain the ceviche mixture through a colander and let it sit for about 15 minutes to drain off the excess liquid as well as to make sure that it's not too cold when you eventually add the compassionate blend and coconut oil.

3. Transfer the ceviche mixture back to a large bowl and use your hands to massage it with the compassionate blend and coconut oil until everything is well coated. Add the tomatillos, onion, dulse flakes, and red chili flakes and mix well. Allow the ceviche to marinate for an additional 30 minutes at room temperature before serving.

4. Make the coconut bacon: Preheat the oven to 250°F. Lightly grease a baking sheet with the coconut oil and set aside.

recipe and ingredients continue

For the Coconut Bacon:

1 teaspoon coconut oil

4 cups dried unsweetened coconut chips

2 tablespoons extra-virgin olive oil

2 teaspoons chipotle powder

1¼ teaspoons Himalayan sea salt

¾ cup maple syrup

For Serving:

Tortilla Chips (see page 41) or store-bought (see Note)

1 small or medium avocado, cubed

2 tablespoons chopped fresh chives

1 lime, cut into wedges

5. In a wide, heavy-bottomed pot over medium-high heat, combine the coconut chips, olive oil, chipotle powder, and salt. Toast for 10 minutes, stirring continuously so the coconut does not burn. When the coconut is a dark golden color, stir in the maple syrup and continue cooking for an additional 2 minutes until the coconut is well coated.

6. Transfer the coconut mixture to the prepared baking sheet and toast in the oven for 10 to 12 minutes, until the chips are dry and crisp. Check in every 3 to 4 minutes and turn the chips over to make sure they cook evenly. Allow them to cool completely. At this point they can be stored in an airtight container or jar for up to 1 month at room temperature.

7. Serve: If you choose to warm your tortilla chips, pop them in the oven for 5 minutes. Place the coconut ceviche in a serving bowl and top with the avocado cubes. Garnish with a generous handful of coconut bacon and the chopped chives. Serve with lime wedges and tortilla chips.

NOTE Warming your tortilla chips in a 250°F oven for 5 minutes before serving is a nice touch and makes this appetizer even more special.

I AM FREE
Beer-Battered Young-Coconut Calamari with Spicy Cocktail Sauce

This fried young-coconut "calamari" is one of those dishes that you can use to convince friends who are skeptical about plant-based eating. It is the perfect storm of crunchy, salty, and fatty and has the added advantage of being gluten-free. We usually serve this with our spicy cocktail sauce, but I also highly recommend blending the sauce (or a store-bought version) with the Cashew Nacho Cheese (page 314) for a creamy, spicy aioli.

SERVES 4

For the Coconut:

8 cups ½-inch-thick strips fresh young Thai coconut (2 or 3 coconuts)

¼ cup fresh lemon juice

1½ teaspoons Himalayan sea salt

½ teaspoon cayenne pepper

½ teaspoon freshly ground black pepper

For the Beer Batter:

1 cup Gluten-Free All-Purpose Bakery Flour Blend (page 34)

1 cup garbanzo flour

2 teaspoons dulse flakes or granules

1 teaspoon Himalayan sea salt

1 teaspoon garlic powder

½ teaspoon cayenne pepper

⅛ teaspoon freshly ground black pepper

1 cup gluten-free beer

1 cup sparkling water

1. Marinate the coconut: In a large bowl, combine the coconut strips, lemon juice, salt, cayenne, and black pepper. Mix well, cover, and marinate overnight in the refrigerator.

2. Make the beer batter: In a large bowl, sift together the gluten-free flour blend and the garbanzo flour. Add the dulse, salt, garlic powder, cayenne, and black pepper and whisk to combine. Pour in the beer and sparkling water and whisk until smooth.

3. Assemble: In a wide, heavy-bottomed saucepan over medium-high heat, heat 2 inches' worth of frying oil. Alternatively, you could do this in an electric fryer. If so, follow the manufacturers' instructions.

4. Heat the oil to 350°F.

5. While the oil heats, remove the marinated coconut from the refrigerator and transfer it to a colander to strain off any excess liquid. Line a plate with a few layers of paper towels and place it next to your frying station.

6. Working in batches, dip the coconut strips in the beer batter, drop them into the hot oil, and fry until they are dark

recipe and ingredients continue

To Assemble:

Rice bran oil or neutral oil of your choice

Himalayan sea salt

Gremolata (page 293) or finely chopped parsley

Spicy Cocktail Sauce (page 306) or store-bought

Lime wedges

golden in color, 1 to 2 minutes. Turn the coconut strips with a fork or slotted spoon as they fry to make sure they are cooked evenly on all sides. Transfer the fried coconut to the paper towel-lined plate to drain, and season with a bit of salt. Repeat with the remaining coconut, bringing the oil back up to temperature in between batches.

7. Garnish the coconut calamari with gremolata or parsley and serve immediately with a side of spicy cocktail sauce and a few wedges of lime to sprinkle.

QUESTION *of the day* / If money were no consideration, what would your life be for?

APPETIZERS & SNACKS

I AM ECSTATIC
Roasted Maple-Miso Brussels Sprouts

This is one of many genius recipes that Ryland Engelhart has contributed to our menus over the years. Ryland is the son of Café Gratitude founders Matthew and Terces Engelhart, and as our mission fulfillment officer, he has the enviable job of keeping the spirit and culture of Café Gratitude alive and well both in the cafés and out in the world. In addition to being one of the most inspired people I know, he has an uncanny ability to create dishes that are tremendously delicious. I Am Ecstatic is a Gratitude mainstay that is eagerly anticipated every year with the return of Brussels sprouts in the fall.

SERVES 4

3 tablespoons maple syrup

2 tablespoons white miso paste

1½ tablespoons apple cider vinegar

2 teaspoons tamari

½ cup extra-virgin olive oil, plus more for the pan

2 pounds fresh Brussels sprouts

1. In a blender, combine the maple syrup, miso paste, apple cider vinegar, and tamari and blend until smooth. Reduce the speed to medium if possible and slowly stream in the ½ cup olive oil, allowing the dressing to emulsify.

2. Preheat the oven to 375°F. Lightly oil a baking sheet and set aside.

3. Remove any tough outer leaves from the Brussels sprouts, trim any discoloration from the bottom of the stem, and cut the sprouts in half.

4. In a large mixing bowl, toss the Brussels sprouts with the maple-miso glaze until they are well coated. Scatter the Brussels sprouts over the oiled baking sheet in a single layer and roast for 25 minutes, checking and turning the sprouts every so often. They should be soft when pierced with a fork, and the glaze will be caramelized and slightly crispy. Serve warm.

I AM FRESH AND BOLD

Cashew Mozzarella and Heirloom Cherry Tomato Skewers with Blackened Tempeh Meatballs

If you are going to be Fresh and Bold, then you will have a beautiful appetizer plate that combines the lightness of Cashew Mozzarella caprese skewers and the vibrant, forward flavor of tempeh meatballs. You could serve them separately and be Fresh or Bold, as we usually are in the cafés, but I think they complement each other naturally as both an affirmation and a flavor combination.

SERVES 4 TO 6

For the Cashew Mozzarella and Heirloom Cherry Tomato Skewers:

1 recipe Gremolata (page 293)

½ cup Cashew Mozzarella (page 312) or store-bought

20 heirloom cherry tomatoes, halved

For the Blackened Tempeh Meatballs:

2 cups sliced shiitake mushrooms

1 medium red beet, cubed

2 tablespoons finely chopped red onion

1 tablespoon balsamic vinegar

1 tablespoon extra-virgin olive oil, plus more if needed

¼ teaspoon Himalayan sea salt

½ cup Coconut Bacon (see page 102) or toasted coconut chips

¼ cup pumpkin seeds, toasted and chopped

1. Make the cashew mozzarella and heirloom cherry tomato skewers: Place the gremolata in a small bowl. Using about 2 teaspoons of cashew mozzarella per ball, roll 20 mozzarella balls with your hands. As you finish rolling, drop and roll the mozzarella in the gremolata so that the entire ball is lightly coated with the herb mixture. Add the finished mozzarella balls to a bowl or a plate.

2. Sandwich each gremolata-crusted mozzarella ball between 2 cherry tomato halves and skewer with a small bamboo skewer or toothpick. Place each finished skewer on a plate or platter and refrigerate until you're ready to serve (the mozzarella will soften at room temperature).

3. Make the blackened tempeh meatballs: Preheat the oven to 400°F.

4. In a large bowl, combine the mushrooms, beets, red onion, balsamic vinegar, olive oil, and salt and toss well to coat. Transfer the mixture to a large baking sheet and roast for 20 to 30 minutes, until the beets are tender. Turn the vegetables frequently and feel free to add a small splash of olive oil if the mixture begins to dry out.

recipe and ingredients continue

1 small garlic clove, chopped

2 cups crumbled soybean tempeh (about 8 ounces)

1 cup lightly packed baby spinach, finely chopped

½ cup cooked steel-cut oats

1 tablespoon fresh parsley, finely chopped

1 tablespoon Compassionate Blend (page 26), optional

1 tablespoon paprika

1 teaspoon smoked salt, plus more for sprinkling

⅛ teaspoon cayenne pepper

⅛ teaspoon chipotle powder

⅛ teaspoon dried thyme

⅛ teaspoon dried oregano

⅛ teaspoon freshly ground black pepper

½ cup white wine for rolling the meatballs (optional)

Rice bran oil or neutral oil of your choice

To Assemble:

1 cup Adobo Buffalo Sauce (page 296), plus more for dipping

2 cups packed arugula

Balsamic Reduction (see page 118), for drizzling

¼ cup Brazil Nut Parmesan (page 317)

5. Allow the vegetables to cool completely, then transfer them to a food processor along with the coconut bacon or coconut chips, pumpkin seeds, and garlic. Pulse the mixture into a rough crumble. Be careful not to overprocess; it should still have some texture.

6. In a large bowl, combine the vegetable mixture, crumbled tempeh, spinach, oats, parsley, compassionate blend, if using, paprika, smoked salt, cayenne, chipotle powder, thyme, oregano, and black pepper. Mix well, then add a third of the mixture back into the food processor and process until the mixture forms a dense, chunky paste. This acts as a nice binder for the meatballs while maintaining the overall texture of the mix.

7. Add the paste mixture back into the bowl and mix well with your hands, making sure all of the ingredients are well distributed.

8. Dampen your hands with the white wine, if desired. In addition to keeping the meatballs from sticking to your hands as you roll, it imparts a nice, subtle flavor. You could also substitute water here. Using approximately 1 tablespoon of mixture per meatball, roll the meatballs with your hands and place them on a large baking sheet.

9. In a wide, heavy-bottomed pot over medium-high heat, add about 2 inches of frying oil. If you are using an electric fryer, follow the manufacturer's instructions. Heat the oil to 350°F. If you don't have a thermometer, you can test the oil by dropping in a small piece of bread. When it floats easily and is covered in foaming oil bubbles, you know the heat is right.

10. Line a plate with paper towels and place it next to your frying station. Fry the meatballs for 3 to 4 minutes, flipping them over halfway through. When the meatballs are crispy and dark brown, transfer them to the lined plate. Sprinkle with smoked salt and skewer with a small bamboo skewer or toothpick. These can be served warm or at room temperature.

recipe continues

11. Assemble: In a small saucepan over low heat, warm the adobo Buffalo sauce.

12. Cover the bottom of a large serving platter with the arugula. This not only lends beautiful color to the dish, it also helps to keep the skewers in place. Arrange the mozzarella and tomato skewers over the arugula and drizzle them with a very light touch of the balsamic reduction. Add the tempeh meatballs to the platter and spoon a little of the warm adobo Buffalo sauce on top of each one. Sprinkle the entire platter generously with the Brazil nut Parmesan and serve.

QUESTION
of the day / What do you give your word to?

I AM ECLECTIC
Flash-Fried Buffalo Cauliflower with Cashew Nacho Cheese

This is not your usual Buffalo cauliflower recipe. Choosing to quickly flash fry rather than breading the cauliflower florets keeps it lighter and really lets the rich sauce play off the creaminess of the cauliflower without interference. By that same token, you can also bake these if you prefer to avoid fried foods. It's delicious either way!

SERVES 4

For the Buffalo Cauliflower:
Rice bran oil or neutral oil of your choice (if frying), or ¼ cup extra-virgin olive oil (if baking)

Adobo Buffalo Sauce (page 296)

2 large heads cauliflower, cut into florets and dried thoroughly

Smoked salt, to taste (if frying), or ½ teaspoon Himalayan sea salt (if baking)

For Serving:
½ cup Cashew Nacho Cheese (page 314)

6 celery stalks, trimmed and cut in half

2 scallions (white and green parts), chopped

1. Make the Buffalo cauliflower. If frying: In a large, heavy-bottomed pot over medium-high heat, or in a countertop electric fryer, heat rice bran oil to measure 2 inches to 350°F.

2. In a small saucepan over low heat, warm the adobo Buffalo sauce. This way it will be ready to toss with the cauliflower as soon as it comes out of the fryer. Line a large sheet pan with paper towels and place it near the frying station. Set a large mixing bowl next to the sheet pan.

3. When the oil is hot, test-fry 1 or 2 pieces of cauliflower to make sure the temperature is right. The cauliflower should quickly become covered with bubbles and gently roll in the oil. Start with a 90-second frying time and adjust up or down as needed until the cauliflower is golden and crisp, working in batches and being sure to keep the oil nice and hot as you work.

4. As the cauliflower finishes frying, turn it onto the lined baking sheet just long enough to absorb any excess oil and sprinkle with smoked salt. Transfer the cauliflower to the large bowl and toss it in enough warmed Buffalo sauce to coat it completely.

5. If baking: Preheat the oven to 400°F.

recipe continues

6. In a large mixing bowl, combine the olive oil, salt, and 1 cup of water. Toss the cauliflower florets in the mixture and turn them out onto a rimmed baking sheet large enough to hold all of the cauliflower in a single layer with plenty of space between the florets. Add all of the water mixture to the tray as well. Bake the cauliflower for 20 to 25 minutes, shaking the tray occasionally so it bakes evenly. The water should steam the cauliflower, and the olive oil will give it a nice golden-brown color.

7. While the cauliflower is baking, warm the Buffalo sauce in a small saucepan over low heat. After the initial 20 to 25 minutes of baking, lightly baste the cauliflower with the sauce. Bake for an additional 5 to 7 minutes, until the sauce has baked onto the cauliflower.

8. Serve: Arrange the dressed Buffalo cauliflower on a (preferably warmed) platter and drizzle it with the cashew nacho cheese. Garnish with the celery sticks and chopped scallions.

I AM PRESENT
Caramelized Red Onion, Roasted Butternut Squash, and Grilled Treviso Radicchio Bruschetta

This is another dish inspired by my time in Venice, Italy. It is a variation of the classic Venetian *saor*, a pickle made with caramelized onions, raisins, and pine nuts, used for centuries to preserve fish and vegetables. The elements are prepared separately to highlight their best qualities, and the saor brings them together in a savory, sweet, and sour marinade. In this dish, the bitterness of the radicchio and the acidic pickling juice of the onions are the perfect contrast to the sweetness of the butternut squash. In the cafés you will find this delicious pickled blend mounded on warm bruschetta that has been smeared with Cashew Mozzarella (page 312) and served with an arugula side salad, but it is also very good served at room temperature over warm polenta, both soft and grilled.

SERVES 8

For the Roasted Butternut Squash and Radicchio Saor:

1½ pounds red onions, peeled and halved

2 pounds butternut squash, peeled, seeded, and cut into ½-inch cubes

¼ cup extra-virgin olive oil, plus more as needed

½ teaspoon Himalayan sea salt, plus more to taste

½ pound Treviso radicchio

½ cup apple cider vinegar

¼ cup white wine

¼ cup coconut sugar

¼ cup raisins

¼ cup pine nuts, lightly toasted

1. Make the roasted butternut squash and radicchio saor: Preheat the oven to 375°F.

2. In a large bowl, soak the onions in cold water to cover for 30 minutes. Drain and slice them into thin half-moons.

3. In a medium bowl, toss the squash with 2 tablespoons of the olive oil and a pinch of salt. Spread the squash over a large baking sheet in a single layer and roast for 15 minutes, or until you can pierce it easily with a knife. Set aside to cool completely.

4. Trim any excess stem from the bottom of the radicchio head(s), making sure to leave just enough to hold the leaves together. Cut the head(s) in half lengthwise and brush each cut side with olive oil.

recipe and ingredients continue

For the Balsamic Reduction:

1 cup balsamic or golden balsamic vinegar

¼ cup coconut nectar

To Assemble:

Sourdough bread, cut into rounds

Cashew Mozzarella (page 312) or store-bought

Pink peppercorns, for garnish (optional)

8 cups lightly packed arugula

2 tablespoons extra-virgin olive oil, plus more for brushing the bread

Himalayan sea salt, to taste

5. If you have a charcoal or gas grill, prepare it for medium-hot grilling. If not, heat a stovetop grill pan or cast-iron skillet over medium-high heat. Lightly oil the grill or pan and lay the radicchio on the grill or pan, cut-side down. Cook for 4 to 6 minutes, until the radicchio is charred and soft on the outside and tender on the inside. Brush the top layer of the radicchio with oil and turn over to cook for an additional 4 minutes, or until you can easily pierce the core with a fork.

6. Lightly salt the radicchio and set it aside to cool. Cut the radicchio into 1-inch-wide strips and set aside.

7. Heat the remaining 2 tablespoons of olive oil in a large, heavy-bottomed skillet over medium heat. Add the onions and the ½ teaspoon of salt and stir briefly. Cover the pan and cook on low heat for 20 to 30 minutes, until the onions are very soft and translucent, stirring occasionally to keep their color consistent. Remove the lid, increase the heat to medium-high, and add the apple cider vinegar, white wine, coconut sugar, and raisins. Cook, uncovered, for an additional 3 minutes, or until the wine and vinegar are mostly reduced. The mixture should be thick and saucy, the raisins plump. Taste, adjust for salt, and let cool for 10 minutes before preparing the pickle.

8. To assemble the pickle, divide each of the three pickle elements into thirds. In the bottom of a small (6-inch x 9-inch) baking dish, layer the first third of the caramelized onions, followed by a third of the grilled radicchio, and then a third of the roasted squash. Sprinkle a third of the toasted pine nuts on top and repeat this layering 2 more times until all of the ingredients are used. Cover and refrigerate for 24 to 48 hours before serving.

9. Make the balsamic reduction: In a small saucepan over high heat, combine the balsamic vinegar and coconut nectar. Bring to a boil, reduce the heat to low, and simmer until the mixture has reduced to about ⅓ cup, about 20 minutes. Set aside to cool. The reduction will thicken as it cools.

10. Assemble: Preheat the oven to 400°F.

11. Brush both sides of the bread slices and place on a baking sheet. Toast for 2 minutes per side, or until they're crisp but not overly dry.

12. Spread an abundant smear of cashew mozzarella over the warm crostini and spoon the butternut squash and radicchio pickle on top of the cheese. Pink peppercorns make a really nice garnish on the pickle, but they are optional.

13. In a medium bowl, toss the arugula with the olive oil and a pinch of salt. Serve the bruschetta on a platter with the fresh arugula salad and finish the plate with a drizzle of balsamic reduction.

QUESTION
of the day

How do you cultivate peacefulness?

SOUPS & SALADS

NOTE Depending on the texture you prefer, there are two ways you can make this: If you would like a very smooth soup, combine all of the cherry tomatoes and strawberries in the blender and proceed with the recipe. It is a very elegant presentation and looks great when you finish it with cashew crème fraiche and a sprinkling of fresh basil. If you prefer a rustic soup that showcases the two fruits in all of their glory, leave 2 cups of each out of the blender, slice them, and mix them back into the pureed base before serving.

I AM ADVENTUROUS
Seasonal Chilled Soups

These soups are a true part of our heritage as a previously raw-food restaurant. Now that we've expanded the menu to include cooked foods, though, they primarily appear on summer menus (as well as in our cleanse program), when a bowl of refreshingly chilled soup is most welcome. That said, the creamier soups such as the Szechuan Carrot (page 128) and Coconut Curry (page 122) would also be delightful in the winter, especially when gently warmed to take the cold edge off of them. Either way, these soups are the perfect way to showcase the full flavor profile of the fruits and vegetables therein because they're shining with their full life force.

Heirloom Cherry Tomato and Strawberry with Cashew Crème Fraiche

SERVES 4

4 cups heirloom cherry tomatoes

4 cups fresh strawberries, hulled

6 large fresh basil leaves, plus more sliced thin for garnish (opal or Thai basil are particularly pretty if they are available in your area)

¼ cup fresh lemon juice

1 Medjool date, pitted

1 tablespoon balsamic vinegar

1½ teaspoons Himalayan sea salt

¼ teaspoon freshly ground black pepper

¼ cup extra-virgin olive oil

¼ cup Cashew Crème Fraiche (page 315), for serving

Grilled or toasted sourdough crostini, for serving (optional)

There is a moment in June in Southern California—as well as in many other places—when the last of the full-flavored, true-season strawberries overlap in the local farmers markets with the earliest of the heirloom cherry tomatoes. Although this window of opportunity may vary depending on where you live, when it does happen, this is the soup you need to make.

1. In a blender, combine the cherry tomatoes, strawberries, basil, lemon juice, date, balsamic vinegar, salt, and pepper and blend until smooth. (Or if going for a more rustic texture, see Note.) With the blender speed at medium, slowly stream in the oil while the blender is running to emulsify the soup. Allow the soup to sit for 15 minutes in the refrigerator to chill well before serving.

2. Divide the soup among 4 chilled bowls and add a dollop of the cashew crème fraiche. Garnish with thinly sliced basil and sourdough crostini, if desired.

Coconut Curry

This is one of the original Café Gratitude raw soup recipes that has stood the test of time. Like every classic, this recipe never goes out of style, and while you could make it all year-round, it has a coziness that usually prompts me to bring it back onto the menu around December to battle the ever-so-frosty Southern California winter.

For the Soup:

5 cups Coconut Milk (page 32) or store-bought

3 tablespoons minced fresh ginger

2 teaspoons chopped garlic

¼ cup fresh lemon or lime juice

¼ cup tamari

2 Medjool dates, pitted

1 tablespoon seeded and chopped jalapeño

1 tablespoon curry powder

1 teaspoon Himalayan sea salt

2 large fresh basil leaves

1 medium avocado, flesh scooped out

½ cup extra-virgin olive oil

For Serving:

1 cup diced fresh tomatoes

1 cup diced cucumber

1 medium avocado, cubed

Fresh cilantro leaves, for garnish

1. Make the soup: Combine the coconut milk, ginger, garlic, lemon juice, tamari, dates, jalapeño, curry powder, salt, basil, and avocado in a high-speed blender and process on high speed until you have a creamy golden soup.

2. Reduce the blender speed to medium and slowly add the olive oil, allowing the soup to emulsify.

3. Serve: Divide the tomatoes, cucumber, and avocado among 4 bowls, pour over the coconut curry soup, and garnish each bowl with a few leaves of cilantro. This soup may be served chilled or blender-warmed.

Honeydew Melon and Cucumber Gazpacho with Spicy Pepitas

SERVES 4

For the Spicy Pepitas:

2 cups pumpkin seeds

¼ cup fresh lime juice

1 teaspoon chipotle powder

¾ teaspoon Himalayan sea salt

¾ teaspoon smoked salt

½ teaspoon chili powder

½ teaspoon cayenne pepper

For the Gazpacho:

5 cups seeded and cubed honeydew melon

3 cups peeled, seeded, and cubed cucumbers

2 scallions (white and green parts), cut into ½-inch pieces

½ cup fresh orange juice

¼ cup fresh lime juice

10 large fresh basil leaves

2 large mint leaves, plus ¼ cup, chopped, for garnish

1 teaspoon Himalayan sea salt

¼ cup extra-virgin olive oil, plus more for drizzling

The alkalinity of the cucumbers is the ideal counterpoint to the sweetness of the melons, and the spicy pumpkin seeds provide a satisfyingly crunchy finale.

1. Make the spicy pepitas: Preheat the oven to 200°F.

2. In a medium bowl, add the pumpkin seeds, lime juice, chipotle powder, sea salt, smoked salt, chili powder, and cayenne. Mix until the pumpkin seeds are well coated, then transfer them to a large baking sheet.

3. Bake for 30 to 40 minutes, until the seeds are dry, mixing frequently so they don't burn. Allow the seeds to cool.

4. Make the gazpacho: In a food processor, pulse the melon just until it is broken down into small chunks. Transfer the melon to a medium bowl and chill in the refrigerator while you continue making the soup.

5. Repeat with the cucumbers, pulsing in the food processor just until it is broken down into small chunks. Transfer half of the pulsed cucumbers and half of the pulsed melons to a blender. Leave the remainder of the cucumbers and melon refrigerated while you make the soup base.

6. Add the scallions, orange juice, lime juice, basil, 2 mint leaves, and salt to the blender. Blend on high speed until the mixture is smooth, then reduce the blender speed to medium and slowly stream in the ¼ cup olive oil until the soup is emulsified.

7. Transfer the soup base to a large bowl and fold in the remaining cucumber and honeydew melon. Chill for at least 15 minutes before serving.

8. Spoon the soup into 4 chilled serving bowls. Garnish with the spicy pepitas, chopped fresh mint, and a drizzle of olive oil.

Szechuan Carrot

SERVES 4

For the Soup:

4 cups fresh carrot juice

1½ cups coconut water (from young Thai coconuts or bottled)

1 cup frozen and thawed young Thai coconut meat

½ large avocado (about ⅓ cup avocado meat)

¼ cup shredded carrots

¼ cup raw cashews

2 Medjool dates, pitted

2 small garlic cloves

One 1-inch knob fresh ginger

2 tablespoons raw sesame tahini

2 tablespoons raw almond butter

2 tablespoons tamari soy sauce

1 tablespoon fresh lemon juice

2 teaspoons sesame oil

¼ teaspoon red chili flakes

For Serving:

1 cup shredded or spiralized carrots

Red chili flakes, to taste

Toasted sesame or extra-virgin olive oil, for drizzling

While this soup is technically raw, the rich creaminess of the tahini, almond butter, and coconut meat interact with the red chilies to make it soothingly warming for late autumn. If you're really lucky, you might even find some late-harvest carrots that have been hit with a touch of early frost to bring out their sweetness.

1. Make the soup: In a blender, combine all of the soup ingredients and blend on high speed until you have a smooth, creamy consistency.

2. Serve: Garnish with a nice mound of shredded or spiralized carrots, a pinch of red chili flakes, and a few drops of toasted sesame or olive oil. This soup may be served chilled or lightly warmed in the blender.

I AM THRIVING

Warm Soups

I'm always amazed by people's devotion to soup because it's such a humble preparation. And yet when done with a little bit of time and care, the end result is a wholesome, warming meal in a bowl. Our classic approach involves sweating down a mirepoix, deglazing with a little white wine, and going from there. Once you get the basics down, you could make pretty much anything.

Curried Red Lentil

SERVES 6

This soup is unexpectedly light, with a tangy citrus finish. It manages to be both cooling in the heat of summer and warming in the winter. In order to preserve the vibrancy of the flavors, make sure that you do not cook this soup for too long once you've added the jalapeño and fresh tomatoes.

For the Soup:

2 tablespoons extra-virgin olive oil

2 tablespoons chopped garlic

2 cups diced yellow onions

1 cup diced celery

1 cup diced carrots

1 tablespoon curry powder

⅓ cup ginger juice or one 1-inch knob fresh ginger blended with ⅓ cup of water

2 cups red lentils

3 cups diced fresh tomatoes

1 tablespoon seeded and finely chopped jalapeño

½ cup fresh lemon juice

½ cup finely chopped fresh cilantro

1 teaspoon Himalayan sea salt

For Serving:

1½ cups diced fresh tomatoes

1 cup chopped fresh cilantro

Extra-virgin olive oil, for drizzling

1. Make the soup: In a large soup pot over medium heat, warm the olive oil. Add the garlic and sauté until the garlic is softened, about 1 minute. Add the onions, celery, carrots, and curry powder and raise the heat to medium-high. Sauté the mixture until the vegetables have softened and their juices have been cooked off, about 5 minutes. Add the ginger juice, lentils, and 8 cups of water and bring to a boil.

2. Reduce the heat to medium-low and partially cover the pot. Keep the soup at an active simmer, stirring occasionally, for 15 to 20 minutes, until the lentils are just tender but not mushy. Add the tomatoes and jalapeño and cook for an additional 5 minutes. Remove the soup from the heat and stir in the lemon juice, cilantro, and salt.

3. Serve: Ladle the soup into 6 warmed serving bowls and garnish each bowl with ¼ cup of diced tomatoes, some chopped cilantro, and a drizzle of olive oil to finish.

White Bean and Lacinato Kale

SERVES 6

This is a classic, rustic soup to make in the late autumn or early winter when lacinato kale is at its peak, though it's just as delightful in warmer months when greens are still readily available. It's enhanced by a small dollop of Basil Hempseed Pesto (page 302) in the summer or Sun-dried Tomato Pesto (page 303) in the winter.

For the Soup:

2 tablespoons extra-virgin olive oil

2 tablespoons chopped garlic

3 cups diced fennel

2 cups diced yellow onions

1 cup diced celery

1½ cups diced carrots

2 tablespoons chopped fresh herbs such as thyme, oregano, or rosemary

⅓ cup white wine

2 cups dried cannellini or white navy beans, soaked overnight, drained, and rinsed

1 bunch lacinato kale, chopped into 1- to 2-inch pieces

1 teaspoon Himalayan sea salt, plus more to taste

½ teaspoon freshly ground black pepper, plus more to taste

For Serving:

Fresh basil leaves, for garnish

Extra-virgin olive oil, for drizzling

Basil Hempseed Pesto (page 302), optional

Sun-dried Tomato Pesto (page 303), optional

1. Make the soup: In a large soup pot over medium heat, warm the olive oil. Add the garlic and cook until softened, about 1 minute. Add the fennel, onions, celery, carrots, and herbs. Raise the heat to medium-high and sauté the vegetables for 5 minutes, or until they are softened and their juices have cooked off.

2. Stir in the white wine and use a wooden spoon to scrape up any flavorful bits from the bottom of the pot. Add the white beans and 8 cups of water and bring the soup to a boil. Reduce the heat to medium-low and partially cover the pot. Keep the soup at an active simmer, stirring occasionally, for 45 minutes, or until the beans are cooked through and the broth is reduced by about a third.

3. Add the chopped kale, salt, and pepper and cook for an additional 5 minutes. Check for seasoning and adjust as you like.

4. Serve: Ladle the soup into 6 warmed bowls and garnish with torn basil leaves and a drizzle of good olive oil. The soup is delicious with a small dollop of the basil hempseed pesto in summer, or sun-dried tomato pesto in winter.

NOTE Dried cannellini beans can sometimes be hard to find, so feel free to use white navy beans. If you don't have time to soak the beans overnight, you can take a shortcut: Cover the beans with water in a saucepan and bring them to a boil. Immediately remove the saucepan from the heat and let the beans sit until they are cool. Discard the soaking water, rinse the beans well, and then proceed with the recipe.

Chipotle Butternut Squash

SERVES 6

2 tablespoons extra-virgin
olive oil

2 tablespoons chopped garlic

2 cups diced yellow onions

1 cup diced celery

1 cup diced carrots

1 cup diced red bell pepper

2 tablespoons chopped fresh
rosemary, plus more for garnish
(optional)

1½ teaspoons chipotle powder

2 tablespoons white wine

6 cups peeled, seeded, and
cubed butternut squash
(about 1 large squash)

⅓ cup raw cashews

⅓ cup fresh orange juice

1 teaspoon Himalayan sea salt,
plus more to taste

Cashew Ricotta (page 311),
for serving (optional)

Chopped fresh cilantro,
for serving (optional)

A cozy, satisfying soup that always graces our fall and winter menus. The cashew ricotta is a nice touch as a garnish, but you could also keep things simple by just sprinkling the soup with chopped cilantro or rosemary.

---

1. In a large soup pot over medium heat, warm the olive oil. Add the garlic and sauté until softened, about 1 minute. Increase the heat to medium-high and add the onions, celery, carrots, pepper, rosemary, and chipotle powder. Sauté until the vegetables have softened and their juices have cooked off, about 5 minutes.

2. Stir in the white wine and use a wooden spoon to scrape up any flavorful bits from the bottom of the pot. When the wine has evaporated, add the squash, turning it over a few times to coat it in the vegetable mixture. Add 6 cups of water, increase the heat to high, and bring the soup to a boil.

3. Reduce the heat to medium-low and partially cover the pot. Keep the soup at an active simmer for 20 to 30 minutes, stirring occasionally, until the squash is soft and the broth is reduced by about a third.

4. Meanwhile in a blender, combine the cashews, orange juice, and salt and blend until completely smooth. Add broth from the soup to loosen, if necessary.

5. Use an immersion blender to blend the soup until it is completely smooth. Or, allow the soup to cool for 15 minutes, then transfer it to a food processor or blender. Process it in batches, working carefully with the hot liquid.

6. Stir in the orange-cashew cream, taste, and adjust for salt.

7. For an even smoother soup with a velvety sheen, pass the pureed soup through a fine-mesh strainer before serving. Ladle the soup into 6 warmed bowls and drizzle on the cashew ricotta, if using, and a generous sprinkle of chopped cilantro or rosemary, if desired.

Mushroom Pozole Verde

SERVES 6 TO 8

15 tomatillos

1½ teaspoons cumin seeds

2 whole dried chipotle peppers

1 cup chopped fresh cilantro
(about 1 bunch)

1 tablespoon Himalayan sea
salt, plus more to taste

2 teaspoons fresh Mexican
oregano

1½ teaspoons dried Mexican
oregano

1 dried hoja santa leaf or
dried bay leaf

½ cup extra-virgin olive oil

½ cup diced yellow onion

3 cups peeled and diced yellow
potatoes

2 cups sliced cremini
mushrooms

2 cups sliced shiitake
mushrooms

¾ cup thinly sliced frozen and
thawed coconut meat

1½ cups cooked chickpeas
(see Note)

1½ cups cooked hominy
(homemade or canned,
drained and rinsed)

Freshly ground black pepper
to taste

Shredded green cabbage,
for serving (optional)

Tortilla Strips, for serving
(page 41) (optional)

Thinly sliced radishes,
for serving (optional)

Avocado slices, for serving
(optional)

Fresh cilantro leaves,
for serving (optional)

Epifanio Ruiz, a longtime Café Gratitude chef who has collaborated with me on many dishes over the years, introduced this plant-based version of a Mexican classic to the menu. The use of traditional ingredients like *hoja santa* and Mexican oregano give this soup an authentic flavor, but if you are unable to source them in your area, you could substitute the hoja santa with bay leaf and use regular oregano instead. At Café Gratitude, we top this soup with shredded green cabbage and fried tortilla strips, but you could dress it up with thinly sliced radish, avocado, and a few leaves of cilantro—whatever speaks to your appetite and inclinations.

---

1. Set a large cast-iron skillet over medium-high heat on the stove. Alternatively you can preheat a grill to medium-high heat. When the pan is smoking hot, add the tomatillos and allow them to char and blister, undisturbed, for about 7 minutes. Turn the tomatillos and repeat on the other side, another 7 minutes. Set aside.

2. In the same large skillet over medium heat, toast the cumin seeds and the chipotles until just fragrant, no more than 2 minutes. Nudge around the cumin and chipotles occasionally to keep them from burning. Set aside to cool.

3. In a blender or food processor, combine the charred tomatillos, toasted cumin seeds and chipotles, cilantro, salt, fresh oregano, dried oregano, hoja santa or bay leaf, and 4 cups of water. Blend until the mixture is smooth, or leave some texture, if you prefer. Transfer to a large bowl. Set aside.

4. In a large skillet over medium heat, warm ¼ cup of the olive oil and add the onion. Cook for 2 minutes, until the onion is softened, then add the potatoes. Cover the pan and cook the potatoes for 5 to 7 minutes, until they are soft, turning them frequently so they cook evenly.

recipe continues

NOTE If you are using canned versions of the chickpeas or hominy, make sure they are unsalted and that they are well drained and rinsed. If you are cooking the chickpeas from scratch, soak ¾ cup of dried chickpeas overnight with 3 cups of water, as they will double in size. The following morning, drain them, cover them with fresh water, and simmer them until they are soft, about 1½ hours. Lightly salt them and let cool, then proceed with the recipe.

5. In a blender or food processor, combine the potato-onion mixture with 3 cups of water. Blend the mixture until it is smooth. Set aside.

6. In a large soup pot over medium heat, warm the remaining ¼ cup olive oil and add the creminis, shiitakes, and coconut. Sauté for 5 minutes, until the mushrooms have softened and just begun to brown. Stir in the chickpeas, hominy, tomatillo mixture, and the potato mixture and bring to a boil. Reduce the heat and simmer, partially covered, until the flavors have come together, about 10 minutes. Taste and season with more salt and pepper, if necessary. Serve with your desired toppings.

QUESTION *of the day* / What are you passionate about?

I AM LUCKY
Mexican Chopped Salad

I had been thinking about doing a chopped salad for years, but for some reason I stood in my own way. I don't know what took me so long, because now it's one of my favorite things on the menu. Feel free to mix and match the ingredients. There's just one guiding principle: You should be able to eat this salad with a spoon, so make sure everything is finely chopped.

This perfect California summer version highlights the special relationship we have with Mexican ingredients. If you can find *verdolagas* ("purslane") or wild edible greens like dandelion greens, mustard greens, and amaranth at your local farmers market, they are great wild-food additions.

SERVES 4

For the Adobo Tempeh:

½ teaspoon Himalayan sea salt, plus more for pot

One 8-ounce block of tempeh

3 whole dried ancho or guajillo chilies

2 small Roma tomatoes, roughly chopped

1 red bell pepper, cored, seeded, and chopped

½ cup chopped yellow onion

3 garlic cloves

3 dried avocado leaves (see page 47) or bay leaves

½ teaspoon whole black peppercorns

½ teaspoon dried oregano

¼ teaspoon cayenne pepper

1 whole clove

2 tablespoons extra-virgin olive oil

1. Make the adobo tempeh: In a medium pot over medium-high heat, combine 4 cups of water and a pinch of salt. Bring the water to a boil and blanch the block of tempeh for 5 minutes. Drain the tempeh and set it aside to cool slightly.

2. In a medium bowl, soak the chilies in warm water until soft, about 10 minutes. Drain the chilies, remove and discard the stems and seeds, and transfer them to a blender. Add the tomatoes, bell pepper, onion, garlic, avocado or bay leaves, ½ teaspoon salt, peppercorns, oregano, cayenne, and clove and blend into a smooth sauce.

3. Cut the tempeh into ½-inch cubes and place them in a shallow bowl or dish. Pour the sauce over the tempeh to cover and marinate in the refrigerator for at least 4 hours and up to overnight.

4. Make the nopales verdes: In a medium pot over medium-high heat, combine 6 cups of water and a pinch of salt. Bring to a boil, add the nopales, and cook for 10 minutes. Drain and place in a medium bowl. Set aside.

recipe and ingredients continue

For the Nopales Verdes:

¾ teaspoon Himalayan sea salt, plus more for pot

2 small nopales (cactus leaves), cleaned and cut into ½-inch squares (see Note)

1 cup roughly chopped fresh cilantro (about 1 bunch)

½ avocado

3 tablespoons fresh lemon juice

2 tablespoons seeded and roughly chopped jalapeño

1 scallion (white and green parts), roughly chopped

1 garlic clove

For the Lucky Vinaigrette:

2 tablespoons apple cider vinegar

1 tablespoon fresh lemon juice

2 teaspoons coconut nectar

1 teaspoon capers in brine, drained

1 garlic clove, chopped

¼ teaspoon Himalayan sea salt

⅛ teaspoon freshly ground black pepper

⅓ cup extra-virgin olive oil

For Serving:

4 cups chopped romaine

4 cups finely chopped kale

1 cup fresh, sweet corn kernels

1 cup cooked chickpeas, homemade (see page 138) or canned

Cilantro Pumpkin Seed Pesto (page 301), optional

Goji Chipotle Dressing (page 278)

Spicy Pepitas (see page 127)

1 cup fried tortilla strips (page 41) or crushed tortilla chips (optional)

4 to 6 squash blossoms (optional)

5. In a blender or food processor, combine the cilantro, avocado, lemon juice, jalapeño, scallion, garlic, and ¾ teaspoon salt with ¾ cup of water, and blend into a smooth, creamy sauce. Pour 1 cup of the sauce over the nopales and toss. (Remaining sauce will keep, covered, in the refrigerator for up to 5 days; use it as a dip or dressing.) In a large skillet over medium heat, cook the dressed nopales until the mixture is heated through, about 2 minutes. Allow the mixture to cool before using in the salad.

6. Make the lucky vinaigrette: In a blender, combine the apple cider vinegar, lemon juice, coconut nectar, capers, garlic, salt, and pepper and blend until smooth. With the blender running on medium speed, slowly drizzle in the olive oil and blend until fully emulsified. Set aside.

7. Drain the tempeh. In a large skillet over medium-high heat, warm the 2 tablespoons of olive oil in a skillet and add the adobo tempeh cubes. Sauté the tempeh until it is lightly blackened, about 10 minutes.

8. Serve: Place the romaine and kale in a large salad bowl and add the nopales, corn, chickpeas, and the lucky vinaigrette. Toss well.

9. Scatter the adobo tempeh over the top of the salad and garnish with small dollops of the cilantro pumpkin seed pesto (if using), a drizzle of the goji chipotle dressing, and a small handful of the spicy pepitas. Finish the salad with tortilla strips and squash blossoms, if you like.

NOTES If you have access to fresh nopales, then the nopales verdes is a great addition to this salad. You can often find them already cleaned of their needles, but double-check that they are completely clean by scraping them with a knife under running water. Use protective gloves or kitchen tongs to hold the nopales as you work.

You'll want to leave time to let the adobo tempeh marinate.

I AM PURE
Asian Kale and Seaweed Salad

This is one of the CG originals. It's been on the menu virtually in this form since its inception, and to this day is among our strongest sellers. It's a classic marinated kale salad that feels like it's never going out of style, and despite all the competition it gets from our other—very delicious—salads, it holds its own. I believe the iron- and mineral-rich sea vegetables are partially to credit, though the creamy, garlicky dressing that's essentially our version of a Green Goddess dressing is what gives this salad its craveable staying power.

SERVES 4

6 cups baby kale, chopped green or purple kale, or a mixture

½ cup diced cucumber

½ cup shredded carrots

½ cup sea palm or wakame, soaked in warm water for 15 minutes and cut into 1-inch pieces

½ cup chopped fresh cilantro, basil, and scallions (any ratio you'd like)

1 sheet of nori, cut into bite-sized strips

¼ cup Garlic Tahini Dressing (page 279)

¼ cup Sesame Wasabi Sauce (page 299)

1 avocado, sliced

½ cup fresh mung bean sprouts

¼ cup toasted almonds, roughly chopped

In a large serving bowl, combine the kale, cucumber, carrots, sea palm, herb mixture, nori, garlic tahini dressing, and sesame wasabi sauce. Toss to ensure everything is evenly coated. Top with the sliced avocado, sprouts, and toasted almonds.

I AM DAZZLING
Kale Caesar Salad with Wakame and Brazil Nut Parmesan

This mainstay from our raw-food days has gotten a major update in the past few years. I added my secret ingredient—a blend of a classic creamy Cashew Caesar Dressing and our Goji Chipotle Dressing for its bright acidity—plus sea vegetables, for a nice, slightly anchovy-style flavor de mar, and capers, for the salty brininess you're looking for in this salad. There are many varieties of kale now available, and all of them would work well.

SERVES 4

For the Garlic Herb Croutons
(or use store-bought):

½ loaf gluten-free sourdough bread of choice, cut into ½-inch cubes (about 2 cups)

2 tablespoons extra-virgin olive oil

1½ teaspoons chopped garlic

1½ teaspoons smoked sea salt

1 teaspoon dried oregano

For Serving:

6 cups finely shredded kale

6 cups finely chopped romaine lettuce

¼ to ½ cup Cashew Caesar Dressing (page 277)

2 tablespoons capers in brine, rinsed

2 tablespoons dry wakame or hijiki seaweed, soaked in cold water for 5 minutes and drained

1 large avocado, cubed

Gomasio (page 27)

Brazil Nut Parmesan (page 317)

1. Make the garlic herb croutons: Preheat the oven to 375°F.

2. In a medium bowl, toss together the bread, 1 tablespoon of the olive oil, the garlic, salt, and oregano. Some bread will absorb more oil than others; if your mixture is still dry, add the remaining 1 tablespoon oil and toss once again. Spread the bread mixture over a baking sheet and bake for 7 to 10 minutes, shaking the pan frequently to shuffle around the bread so it crisps evenly. The croutons should be golden brown.

3. Serve: In a large bowl, toss together the kale and romaine along with the Caesar dressing. Add 1 tablespoon of the capers, half of the croutons, and the rehydrated wakame or hijiki.

4. Transfer the salad to a serving dish. Garnish with the avocado, the remaining 1 tablespoon capers and croutons, and a generous sprinkle of the gomasio and Brazil nut Parmesan.

I AM LOCAL

Our menu wouldn't be complete without a simple salad offering that reflected what was freshest at the market. Each preparation allows the seasonal elements to really shine.

Autumn:

Shaved Kale, Persimmon, and Pomegranate Salad with Fig Balsamic Dressing

SERVES 4

For the Maple Walnuts:
1 cup raw walnuts

1 teaspoon maple syrup

⅛ teaspoon Himalayan sea salt

For the Salad:
6 cups stemmed and shredded kale

2 cups shredded radicchio

½ cup shaved or very thinly sliced fennel

1 cup Fig Balsamic Dressing (page 282)

1 ripe Fuyu persimmon, cut into ½-inch cubes

½ cup pomegranate seeds

¼ cup crumbled Cashew Mozzarella (page 312)

Some people will grill persimmons to draw out their sweetness, but here I suggest using them in their most natural state (all the more reason to let them fully ripen!). They are a mellower companion to the tartness of the pomegranate, offset by the vegetal radicchio and kale. This salad truly is a last breath of freshness as you head into the winter season.

1. Make the maple walnuts: Preheat the oven to 375°F. Line a baking sheet with parchment paper.

2. In a large bowl, combine the walnuts, maple syrup, and salt and mix thoroughly to coat the nuts. Spread the mixture over the baking sheet and bake for 20 minutes. Let the walnuts cool completely.

3. Make the salad: In a large bowl, combine the kale, radicchio, fennel, and fig balsamic dressing. Toss for a minute or two to soften the vegetables.

4. Arrange the dressed salad in a large serving bowl or on a platter and top with the persimmon, pomegranate seeds, the maple walnuts, and cashew mozzarella.

Grilled Peach and Asparagus Salad with Spicy Pepitas, Cashew Mozzarella, and Goji Chipotle Dressing

SERVES 4

Himalayan sea salt, to taste

16 medium asparagus spears

4 large peaches

Extra-virgin olive oil, for grilling

6 cups arugula

6 cups baby spinach

1 cup shaved or very thinly sliced fennel

¼ cup cashew mozzarella, for serving

1 recipe Goji Chipotle Dressing (page 278)

Spicy Pepitas (see page 127)

Gremolata (page 293)

Coconut Bacon (see page 102), optional

At the peak of summer, this makes a beautiful entrée salad for lunch or a first course for dinner. It's the ideal backdrop against which to showcase perfectly ripe peaches, but the grill will turn even a slightly green peach into a sweet, smoky nugget by caramelizing the sugars.

1. In a medium pot over medium-high heat, bring 6 cups of lightly salted water to a boil. Fill a large bowl with ice water and set aside. Once the water is at a rolling boil, blanch the asparagus for 3 minutes, until it's bright green and tender but still crisp. Immediately transfer the asparagus to the ice water. Let the asparagus cool in the water for 1 minute before transferring it to a plate. Pat the asparagus dry with a paper towel and set aside.

2. Preheat an outdoor grill or stovetop grill pan to medium-high heat.

3. Cut the peaches into ¼- to ½-inch-thick slices. Brush the peaches and asparagus with olive oil and arrange them on the grill. Cook until the peaches have softened slightly, and both the peaches and asparagus have nice grill marks, about 2 minutes per side. Remove the peaches and asparagus from the grill and set aside.

4. In a large mixing bowl, toss together the arugula, spinach, and shaved fennel. Arrange the greens on a large serving plate and place the grilled peaches and asparagus on top. Add pieces of crumbled cashew mozzarella, a drizzle of the goji chipotle dressing, and a sprinkling of spicy pepitas and gremolata. Finish with coconut bacon, if desired.

Warm Brussels Sprouts Salad with Capers, Coconut Bacon, and Hempseed Ranch Dressing

SERVES 4

1 pound Brussels sprouts, stems trimmed and outer leaves removed

1 tablespoon extra-virgin olive oil

1 teaspoon Himalayan sea salt

1 pound baby spinach

¼ cup capers in brine, drained

1 cup Purple Cabbage Kimchi (page 320)

1 cup Creamy Hempseed Ranch Dressing (page 283)

½ cup Goji Chipotle Dressing (page 278)

1 cup Coconut Bacon (see page 102)

¼ cup dried golden berries

1 avocado, diced

This is the Gratitude interpretation of the classic warm bacon salad. The coconut bacon—a very worthy pantry staple that gets put to use in a number of our recipes—really emulates the sweet, fatty, spicy, smoky flavor of its traditional counterpart. Combined with the warm shaved Brussels sprouts, spinach, and creamy dressing, this is the ultimate comforting winter salad.

1. Using a mandoline or a food processor with the slicing attachment, thinly shred the Brussels sprouts.

2. Heat the olive oil in a large skillet over medium-high heat. Add the Brussels sprouts and salt and sauté, stirring frequently, until the sprouts are tender but retain some bite, about 10 minutes.

3. In a large serving bowl, combine the warm sprouts with the spinach, capers, kimchi, hempseed ranch, and goji chipotle dressing. Mix until everything is well dressed and combined. Garnish with the coconut bacon, golden berries, and diced avocado.

I AM GRACIOUS

The grain salad has a permanent place on our menu and is for anyone who wants the nourishing, satisfying quality of whole grains but in a fresh, light salad context. I'm particularly fond of a grain foundation, as it's the perfect canvas for getting inspired by the colors of the seasons. There are endless variations and possibilities, so feel free to riff on this construction however you like.

Summer:

Avocado, Green Beans, and Basil Hempseed Pesto

SERVES 4

1 teaspoon Himalayan sea salt

½ pound green beans, trimmed and roughly chopped

4 cups arugula

1 cup cooked grain of your choice, such as quinoa or brown rice (or a mixture, if desired)

1 avocado, cubed

6 cherry tomatoes, halved

½ cup diced cucumber

¼ cup Basil Hempseed Pesto (page 302)

Juice of 1 lemon

2 tablespoons Brazil Nut Parmesan (page 317)

2 tablespoons crumbled Cashew Mozzarella (page 312)

2 teaspoons Balsamic Reduction (see page 118)

A light summer warm-weather offering dotted with hues of vibrant green.

1. In a medium bowl, prepare an ice water bath and place it near the stove.

2. In a medium pot over high heat, bring 4 cups of water to a boil. Add the salt and stir to dissolve. Add the green beans and cook for 3 minutes, or until the green beans are tender but still have some bite. Drain the green beans and immediately plunge them into the ice bath. Allow them to cool for a few minutes, then drain thoroughly and transfer to a large serving bowl.

3. Combine the green beans with the arugula, cooked grain, avocado, tomatoes, cucumber, pesto, and lemon juice. Toss thoroughly to combine. Top with the Parmesan and mozzarella and drizzle with the balsamic reduction.

Radicchio, Roasted Butternut Squash, and Sun-dried Tomato Pesto

The rusty tones of winter bring warmth and subtle sweetness to this dish.

SERVES 4

1 cup peeled, seeded butternut squash, cut into 1-inch cubes

1 teaspoon extra-virgin olive oil

¼ teaspoon Himalayan sea salt

4 cups shredded radicchio

1 cup cooked grain of your choice, such as quinoa or brown rice (or a mixture, if desired)

½ cup cooked chickpeas, homemade (see page 138) or canned

¼ cup Sun-dried Tomato Pesto (page 303)

6 black sun-dried olives or oil-cured olives, pitted and roughly chopped

2 teaspoons capers in brine, drained

2 tablespoons Brazil Nut Parmesan (page 317)

2 tablespoons crumbled Cashew Mozzarella (page 312)

2 teaspoons Balsamic Reduction (see page 118)

1. Preheat the oven to 375°F. Line a baking sheet with parchment paper.

2. In a medium bowl, toss the squash with the olive oil and salt until the squash is evenly coated with the oil. Spread the squash over the baking sheet and bake for 20 to 25 minutes, until it can easily be pierced with a knife or fork. Set aside to cool.

3. In a large serving bowl, combine the cooled squash, radicchio, cooked grain, chickpeas, pesto, olives, and capers. Toss thoroughly to combine. Top with the Parmesan and mozzarella and drizzle with the balsamic reduction.

SANDWICHES
& WRAPS

I AM AWESOME
Baked Eggplant Parmesan Sandwich

Ryland is one of Matthew and Terces Engelhart's sons and is currently serving as our chief inspiration officer. While Ryland's main role includes preserving the original integrity of the Café Gratitude mission as well as finding new, innovative ways for us to achieve higher standards in sustainability, he is also a welcome contributor to our menu. This menu staple is one of his enduring creations, a play on the traditional eggplant parm that he fondly remembers ordering as a young vegetarian (it was often the only vegetarian-friendly item on the menu). Ours is a baked version that avoids the heaviness of fried eggplant, using a simple cornmeal breading to achieve the same sumptuous quality. Topped with our (vegan friendly) ricotta and Parmesan, this sandwich is as delectable as it is easy to prepare at home.

MAKES 6 SANDWICHES

For the Baked Eggplant:
2 cups Fig Balsamic Dressing (page 282)

2 cups fine-ground cornmeal

½ cup dried Italian herb seasoning

1½ tablespoons Himalayan sea salt

1 tablespoon freshly ground black pepper

1 medium eggplant (about 1 pound), sliced into ½-inch-thick rounds

To Assemble:
6 ciabatta or Italian rolls, sliced in half

1 cup Marinara Sauce (page 212) or store-bought, plus more as needed

½ cup Cashew Ricotta (page 311)

1½ cups baby arugula

½ cup Brazil Nut Parmesan (page 317)

1. Make the baked eggplant: Preheat the oven to 350°F. Line a baking sheet with parchment paper and set aside.

2. Pour the dressing into a wide, shallow dish or bowl. Combine the cornmeal, Italian seasoning, salt, and pepper in another wide, shallow dish or bowl.

3. Dip each eggplant slice in the dressing, then dredge and coat thoroughly in the cornmeal mixture. Lay the coated eggplant slices on the lined baking sheet in a single layer and repeat until all of the eggplant is on the baking sheet.

4. Bake the eggplant for 20 minutes, or until the breading has crisped and the eggplant feels soft in the middle.

5. Assemble the sandwiches: Layering from the bottom of the rolls, place 1 or 2 slices of eggplant, a few tablespoons of the marinara, a thin layer of the ricotta, a small handful of the baby arugula, and a sprinkle of the Brazil nut Parmesan. Add the top halves of the rolls and cut the sandwiches in half, if desired.

I AM GLORIOUS
Tempeh Caesar Wrap

In my mind, a great wrap offers everything you need and want in a meal, but all bundled up into a perfect handheld package. Though I'm slightly biased, I think this embodies that mission to a T with its spicy blackened tempeh, smoky coconut bacon, and fresh tomato, all draped in a creamy Caesar dressing and wrapped up in a soft whole-wheat tortilla.

MAKES 4 WRAPS

4 large whole-wheat tortillas

4 cups shredded romaine

1 recipe Blackened Tempeh (see page 48), cut into ¼-inch cubes

1 cup diced fresh tomato

1 avocado, cubed

½ cup Cashew Caesar Dressing (page 277)

1 cup Coconut Bacon (see page 102)

1 tablespoon plus 1 teaspoon capers in brine, drained

¼ cup Brazil Nut Parmesan (page 317)

1. In a large skillet over medium heat, warm the tortillas until soft and pliable, about 1 minute per side. Stack the tortillas on a plate under a kitchen towel to keep them warm as you assemble the wraps. Keep the skillet nearby for griddling the wraps once assembled.

2. In the middle of each tortilla, layer equal amounts of the romaine, tempeh, tomato, avocado, a drizzle of dressing, coconut bacon, capers, and Parmesan. Roll each up into a burrito shape and place back into the skillet, seam-side down, to seal and warm the wraps, about 30 seconds. Serve warm.

I AM EXTRAORDINARY
BLT Sandwich

I inherited this recipe from one of the original Café Gratitude menus, and while it's a familiar idea—bacon, lettuce, and tomato is pretty much the gold standard of sandwiches—it certainly is satisfying. Especially because it delivers the classic flavors and fresh summer experience but with a completely plant-based twist.

MAKES 4 SANDWICHES

4 ciabatta rolls, halved

2 cups Coconut Bacon
(see page 102)

4 cups shredded romaine
lettuce

2 cups diced fresh tomatoes

1 cup Cashew Nacho Cheese
(page 314)

2 avocados, cubed

Creamy Mexican Coleslaw
(see page 175), optional

1. In a large skillet over medium heat, warm each ciabatta slice until lightly toasted, about 1 minute per side. Stack the slices on a plate under a kitchen towel to keep them warm as you assemble the sandwiches.

2. In the center of each bottom ciabatta slice, place ½ cup of the coconut bacon, 1 cup of the shredded romaine, ½ cup of the tomatoes, about ¼ cup of the nacho cheese, and a quarter of the cubed avocado. Top with the second slice of ciabatta bread and serve.

I AM MAGICAL
Gratitude "Double Double" Burger

When we started putting cooked food on the menu, the veggie burger was one of the first items that we of course had to have. But I noticed that during the first couple of years it was on the menu, it wasn't moving. So I decided to really dig in and turn what was—admittedly—a ho-hum burger into the incredible, undeniably magical indulgence that it is now, topped with creamy macadamia Cheddar, spicy chipotle ketchup, and all the veggie fixin's of choice.

This burger does call for a number of ingredients, but the ingredients are easy to come by. And once you make a batch, you can freeze the patties and cook them to order.

SERVES 4

For the Veggie Burgers:

1¼ cups chopped beet (about 1 medium beet)

3 tablespoons extra-virgin olive oil, plus more for the pan

1½ teaspoons smoked salt

1 pound cremini mushrooms, halved

2 tablespoons chopped fresh parsley

1 garlic clove, finely chopped

½ cup cooked black beans, homemade (see page 45) or canned, plus 1 tablespoon of their liquid

⅔ cup pumpkin seeds, toasted

⅓ cup cooked steel-cut oats

⅓ cup cooked quinoa

⅓ cup cooked short-grain brown rice

1 tablespoon ground flaxseeds

1. Make the veggie burgers: Preheat the oven to 350°F. Line 2 baking sheets with parchment paper.

2. In a medium bowl, toss the beet with 1 tablespoon of the olive oil and ½ teaspoon of the smoked salt. Spread the beet over one of the baking sheets.

3. In the same bowl, toss the mushrooms with the parsley, garlic, remaining 2 tablespoons of olive oil, and ½ teaspoon of the smoked salt. Spread over the second baking sheet.

4. Roast the vegetables for 45 minutes to 1 hour, until they are soft and caramelized. (If your oven has a convection feature, this is a great occasion to use it and cut your baking time by 15 minutes or more.) Set aside.

5. In a large bowl, roughly mash the black beans and their liquid using a fork. Leave about a third of the beans whole. Set aside.

6. In a food processor, process ⅓ cup of the pumpkin seeds until they reach the consistency of coarse meal. Add the ground pumpkin seeds to the bowl with the black beans,

recipe and ingredients continue

1 tablespoon Barbecue Sauce (page 307) or store-bought

2 teaspoons Compassionate Blend (page 26), optional

To Assemble:

4 hamburger buns, gluten-free, if desired

½ cup Cashew Nacho Cheese (page 314)

½ cup Chipotle Ketchup (page 306) or store-bought ketchup, plus more for dipping

4 thin slices red onion

1 large tomato, thinly sliced into 4 rounds

Pickles (optional)

1 cup shredded romaine

¼ cup Macadamia Cheddar (page 316)

Roasted Garnet Yams (see page 185)

along with the remaining whole pumpkin seeds, roasted beet and mushrooms, oats, quinoa, brown rice, ground flaxseeds, barbecue sauce, remaining ½ teaspoon of smoked salt, and the compassionate blend, if using. Mix thoroughly to combine. Chill the burger mixture for 1 hour before forming into patties.

7. To form the burgers, use about ⅓ cup of the mixture for each patty, for 8 patties total. Using your hands or 2 sheets of parchment paper, flatten each patty to about 5 inches in diameter.

8. In a large skillet over medium-high heat, heat enough olive oil to very thinly coat the bottom of the pan. When the oil is very hot, carefully place 2 or 3 patties in the pan (to avoid overcrowding). Cook for 3 to 4 minutes per side, until the burgers are a deep golden brown. Add more oil to the pan if needed and continue cooking the remaining burgers.

9. Assemble: On the bottom of each burger bun, spread about 2 tablespoons of the nacho cheese. Top with a burger patty, followed by 1 tablespoon of the ketchup, an onion round, and a slice of tomato. Place a second burger patty on top, followed by another tablespoon of ketchup, pickles (if using), and ¼ cup of romaine. Spread the top bun with a tablespoon of the macadamia cheddar and place it on top of the burger. Serve with garnet yams and additional ketchup for dipping.

I AM ORIGINAL
SF Mission Burrito

Café Gratitude was born in the San Francisco Mission District, and one of my favorite foods in that neighborhood is the taqueria burrito. At the time, I had yet to come across anywhere that did vegan burritos in quite the same way, with the ample rice, beans, and other toppings bundled in a soft tortilla and the signature wrapping of foil. When I decided to re-create the mission-style burrito for the menu, I really wanted to come up with something that emulated a classic carnitas. Through trial and error, I landed on this really incredible version that uses oyster mushrooms. The carnitas is now a staple, offering an elegant solution for so many different traditional dishes beyond Mexican—including Korean and American barbecue. We even use it in our cleanse-friendly salads because it so perfectly and cleanly gives you the sensation of a nice, chewy protein. For this dish, we top the carnitas with our house-made Guacamole, adobo, pico de gallo, and cashew nacho cheese, but you could also load up the carnitas over a bowl of rice—much like our Gratitude Bibimbap Bowl (page 190)—and call it a meal.

MAKES 6 BURRITOS

For the Pico de Gallo:

2 cups chopped fresh tomatoes

¾ cup chopped seedless cucumber or tomatillos

2 scallions (white and green parts), chopped

¼ cup chopped red onion

¼ cup chopped fresh cilantro

2 tablespoons Salsa Verde (page 297)

2 tablespoons fresh lemon juice

½ teaspoon Himalayan sea salt

½ teaspoon freshly ground black pepper

1. Make the pico de gallo: In a large bowl, combine the tomatoes, cucumber, scallions, onion, cilantro, salsa verde, lemon juice, salt, and pepper. Mix thoroughly and set aside.

2. Make the burritos: Heat the olive oil in a large skillet over medium heat. Add the mushroom carnitas and sauté until the mushrooms are crisp, 3 to 5 minutes. Set aside.

3. In a medium skillet over medium heat, warm the tortillas for about 1 minute per side. Stack the tortillas on a plate under a kitchen towel to keep them warm and pliable as you assemble the wraps. Keep the skillet nearby for griddling the burritos.

recipe and ingredients continue

SANDWICHES & WRAPS

169

For the Burritos:

1 tablespoon extra-virgin olive oil

Mushroom Carnitas (see page 175)

6 large whole-wheat tortillas

2 cups cooked brown rice

1½ cups Mexican Black Beans (see page 45)

1 cup Cashew Nacho Cheese (page 314)

½ cup Adobo de Mixiote (page 291)

½ cup Guacamole (page 289)

Tortilla Chips (see page 41) or store-bought, for serving (optional)

Roasted Tomatillo Sauce (page 295), for serving (optional)

4. Down the center of each tortilla, layer the rice, black beans, warmed mushroom carnitas, a spoonful of nacho cheese, some adobo de mixiote, some pico de gallo, and a dollop of guacamole. Roll up the burritos and place them back in the warm skillet, seam-side down, to seal them, about 30 seconds.

5. Serve with some tortilla chips, more pico de gallo, and roasted tomatillo sauce, if you'd like.

QUESTION *of the day* / If you could change one thing in your life, what would that be?

I AM FUERTE
Mexican Torta

This is a classical torta in the sense that it's a big fat sandwich loaded with our traditionally marinated and chorizo-spiced tempeh plus avocado, tomato, cashew nacho cheese, cilantro pesto, and Roasted Tomatillo Sauce. We pile these things high on Mexican *bolillos*—baguette-like rolls—but you could easily use ciabatta or your favorite bread.

MAKES 4 SANDWICHES

Tempeh Chorizo (page 29), up through refrigerating overnight

1 tablespoon extra-virgin olive oil, plus more as needed

4 bolillos or ciabatta rolls, split, or 8 slices bread of your choice, toasted

¼ cup Cilantro Pumpkin Seed Pesto (page 301)

¼ cup Roasted Tomatillo Sauce (page 295)

1 large tomato, sliced

4 large leaves butter or Bibb lettuce

1 avocado, sliced

¼ cup Cashew Nacho Cheese (page 314)

Creamy Mexican Coleslaw (see page 175), optional

Escabeche (page 319), optional

1. Form the chorizo into four 4- to 5-inch patties.

2. In a large skillet over medium-high heat, heat the olive oil. Pan-fry the patties until they are warmed through and slightly brown and crisp, about 2 minutes per side. Add a little more oil to the pan if the patties begin to stick. Transfer the patties to a plate.

3. On the bottom half of each roll or slice of bread, spread 1 tablespoon of the cilantro pesto and 1 tablespoon of tomatillo sauce, followed by a chorizo patty. Top with the sliced tomato, a lettuce leaf, and ¼ of the avocado. Spread the top half of the roll or bread slice with 1 tablespoon of the nacho cheese. Serve with Mexican coleslaw and/or escabeche, if you'd like.

I AM COMMITTED
Pulled Mushroom Sandwich

When you have mushroom carnitas as delicious as ours, it feels like you absolutely have to offer a version of a pulled pork—or pulled mushroom—sandwich to accentuate everything that is amazing about them. The addition of the coleslaw here gives the sandwich a fun Southern twist and adds a welcome crunch to the barbecue-style richness of the carnitas.

MAKES 6 SANDWICHES

For the Mushroom Carnitas:
2½ pounds oyster mushrooms

2 tablespoons extra-virgin olive oil

1 tablespoon chopped garlic

½ teaspoon Himalayan sea salt

¼ cup Adobo de Mixiote (page 291)

For the Creamy Mexican Coleslaw:
4 cups thinly shredded cabbage (red, green, or a mix)

½ cup Cashew Nacho Cheese (page 314)

1 large carrot, shredded

1 scallion (white and green parts), thinly sliced

2 tablespoons chopped fresh cilantro

½ teaspoon Himalayan sea salt

To Assemble:
¼ cup extra-virgin olive oil

12 slices sourdough bread, or your favorite bread

1 cup Chipotle Ketchup (page 306)

1. Make the mushroom carnitas: Preheat the oven to 400°F.

2. Using your fingers, tear the mushrooms into thin shreds. If there are any tiny mushrooms, you can leave them whole.

3. In a large bowl, toss the mushrooms with the olive oil, garlic, and salt. Massage the mushrooms until they're well coated and slightly softened.

4. Spread the mushrooms in one even layer over a baking sheet. Use 2 sheets if necessary to avoid overcrowding the mushrooms. Roast for 12 to 15 minutes, until the mushrooms are dried and slightly crispy. Set aside the mushrooms to cool. Once they're cool enough to handle, roughly chop the mushrooms.

5. In a medium bowl, combine the chopped mushrooms with the adobo de mixiote and toss to coat. Cover and transfer to the refrigerator to marinate overnight.

6. Make the creamy Mexican coleslaw: In a large bowl, combine the cabbage, nacho cheese, carrot, scallion, cilantro, and salt. Massage the mixture gently with your hands to coat the cabbage thoroughly. Cover and refrigerate the coleslaw for 30 minutes to marinate and soften.

recipe and ingredients continue

1 cup Adobo Buffalo Sauce
(page 296)

½ cup Barbecue Sauce
(page 307)

¼ cup chopped fresh cilantro

½ cup Cashew Nacho Cheese
(page 314)

7. Assemble the sandwiches: Preheat a grill, grill pan, or heavy skillet over medium-high heat.

8. Brush the olive oil evenly over the bread slices and grill the bread for a minute or 2 on each side. Set aside.

9. In a large skillet over medium-high heat, add the mushroom carnitas, ketchup, and Buffalo sauce. Stir to combine and heat until the mixture is slightly reduced and warmed through, 2 to 3 minutes.

10. For each sandwich, spread about a tablespoon of barbecue sauce on the bottom slice of bread. Top with about ½ cup of the warmed carnitas, a small mound of coleslaw, and a sprinkle of cilantro. Spread the top slice of bread with a thick layer of cashew nacho cheese and place on top of the sandwich. Serve warm.

I AM GRACEFUL
Roasted Cherry Tomato, Shiitake Mushroom, and Cashew Mozzarella Tartine

It wasn't until recently that we offered an open-faced sandwich, after I realized how simple a preparation it would be for our kitchen: You can make all the components in advance, assemble the sandwiches, pop them into the oven or under the broiler, and have a delicious savory lunch. The original reference for this version was a French tartine, with cured meats, cheese, and pesto. We replace the meats with simply cooked yet hearty vegetables, add our Cashew Mozzarella, and tie it all together with deeply flavorful Sun-dried Tomato Pesto. This tartine is a particularly lovely showpiece for brunches or any other occasion when lunch is served.

SERVES 4

1 pound cherry tomatoes, halved

2 tablespoons extra-virgin olive oil, plus more for sandwiches

½ teaspoon Himalayan sea salt

2 cups arugula

½ teaspoon smoked salt

4 thick slices good sourdough bread (gluten-free, if desired), toasted

¼ cup Sun-dried Tomato Pesto (page 303) or Basil Hempseed Pesto (page 302)

¼ cup crumbled Cashew Mozzarella (page 312)

1. Preheat the oven to 375°F and line a baking sheet with parchment paper.

2. In a medium bowl, toss the cherry tomatoes with 1 tablespoon of the olive oil and the salt. Spread the tomatoes over the baking sheet and roast for 15 to 20 minutes, until they begin to char slightly along the edges. Remove the tomatoes but leave the oven on and reduce the temperature to 350°F.

3. In a medium sauté pan over medium-high heat, heat the remaining tablespoon of olive oil. Add the arugula and smoked salt and sauté briefly until the arugula is just wilted, about 3 minutes. Set aside.

4. Place the toasted bread on a baking sheet and brush each slice with olive oil. Spread evenly with the pesto and divide the wilted arugula among the toasts. Arrange about 6 cherry

recipe and ingredients continue

Braised Mushrooms
(see page 213)

¼ cup Lucky Vinaigrette
(see page 141), plus more
for optional side salad

¼ cup Cashew Ricotta
(page 311)

2 tablespoons Brazil Nut
Parmesan (page 317)

1½ tablespoons Gremolata
(page 293)

8 cups mixed greens, optional

4 Bistro Pickled Carrots
(page 323), cut in half
(optional)

tomato halves on each slice, followed by about a tablespoon of the mozzarella. Top with the braised mushrooms and drizzle with the vinaigrette and ricotta.

5. Bake the tartines for 5 to 7 minutes, until the mozzarella is lightly browned. Cut each tartine into 3 slices, if you like, or leave whole. Garnish with Parmesan and gremolata. If desired, make a quick side salad with the salad greens and ¼ cup more of the vinaigrette, divide among the plates, and serve with the pickled carrots.

QUESTION
of the day / What would you love to be
acknowledged for?

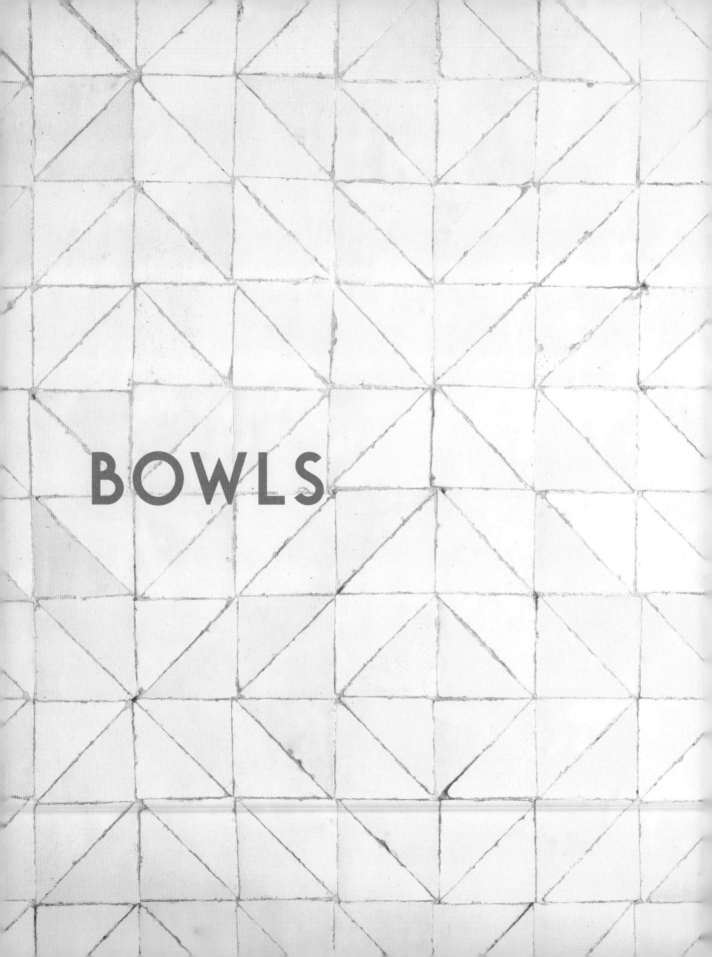

BOWLS

I AM WHOLE
Macrobiotic Bowl

This is the Gratitude iteration of the classic macrobiotic bowl, which is traditionally a healing blend of brown rice, sautéed greens, sea vegetables, adzuki beans, a cooked root vegetable, a ferment, and a garlic tahini dressing. Ours hasn't strayed too far since its initial offering on our original raw menu, though it has evolved as the intention of our menu has evolved—namely including cooked foods. It has consistently been our number-one selling bowl, and there's no mystery why: It's as balancing as it is nourishing; a complete meal in one bowl.

SERVES 4

For the Stewed Adzuki Beans:
1 large garlic clove

1 tablespoon extra-virgin olive oil

2 cups dried adzuki beans, soaked overnight, drained, and rinsed

2 tablespoons tamari

2 tablespoons maple syrup

1 dried bay leaf

1 teaspoon chopped fresh rosemary

1 teaspoon Himalayan sea salt

½ teaspoon dried thyme

½ teaspoon kombu powder

For the Braised Garnet Yams:
4 cups garnet yams, cut into 1-inch cubes

¾ teaspoon Himalayan sea salt

2 teaspoons extra-virgin olive oil

½ cup finely chopped red onion

1. Make the stewed adzuki beans: In a small bowl, mash together the garlic and the olive oil.

2. In a large pot over medium-high heat, combine the soaked adzuki beans, tamari, maple syrup, bay leaf, rosemary, salt, thyme, kombu, and 6 cups of water. Stir in the garlic–olive oil mixture and bring to a boil. Reduce the heat to low and partially cover the pot. Simmer the beans for about 1 hour, until the beans are soft and brothy. Discard the bay leaf.

3. Make the braised garnet yams: In a large pot over medium-high heat, combine the cubed yams with ¾ cup of water and ½ teaspoon of the salt. Bring to a boil and reduce the heat to low. Partially cover the pot and simmer the yams for 30 minutes, stirring occasionally, until the pieces are soft and have partially broken down.

4. While the yams cook, heat the olive oil in a medium skillet over medium heat. Add onion and the remaining ¼ teaspoon of salt and cook until the onion has caramelized, about 10 minutes. Stir into the cooked yams.

recipe and ingredients continue

1 tablespoon extra-virgin olive oil

1 teaspoon chopped garlic

4 cups chopped lacinato kale

1 tablespoon white wine

½ teaspoon Himalayan sea salt

1½ cups cooked grain, such as brown rice or quinoa

1 cup Garlic Tahini Dressing (page 279)

1 cup Purple Cabbage Kimchi (page 320)

1 cup sea palm or wakame, soaked in warm water for 15 minutes and cut into 1-inch pieces

1 cup sunflower seed sprouts, broccoli sprouts, or alfalfa sprouts

½ cup toasted chopped almonds

1½ tablespoons Gomasio (page 27)

5. Serve: In a large skillet over medium-high heat, heat the olive oil. Add the garlic and cook until just golden, no more than 30 seconds. Add the kale and cook for 3 minutes, or until the kale has mostly wilted. Add the white wine and salt, stirring and turning the kale for another minute, just until the alcohol has cooked off.

6. In individual bowls, layer the cooked grain, the sautéed kale, a scoop of adzuki beans, and a scoop of braised yams. Top with the garlic tahini dressing, kimchi, and the soaked sea vegetables. Garnish with the sprouts, toasted almonds, and a sprinkle of gomasio.

QUESTION *of the day* / Whom could you acknowledge?

I AM HUMBLE
Indian Curry Bowl

Another Gratitude essential that was created by Ryland Engelhart. It's a classic Indian red daal that's made even more delicious with our spicy tomato jam and mint-coconut chutney. Its simplicity is matched only by how satisfying and delicious it is.

SERVES 4

For the Curried Lentils:
2½ cups dried red lentils

1¼ cups Coconut Milk (page 32) or store-bought

1 tablespoon chopped fresh ginger

1½ teaspoons Himalayan sea salt

1¼ teaspoons curry powder

½ teaspoon cumin

½ teaspoon turmeric

½ teaspoon cayenne pepper

2 tablespoons extra-virgin olive oil

½ cup chopped yellow onion

1 tablespoon chopped garlic

¼ cup tamari soy sauce

1½ tablespoons coconut butter or coconut manna

For the Vegetables:
2 garnet yams, cut into ½-inch-thick half-moons

3 tablespoons extra-virgin olive oil

2 teaspoons Himalayan sea salt

8 cups loosely packed baby spinach

1. Make the curried lentils: In a large pot over medium-high heat, combine 5 cups of water, the lentils, coconut milk, ginger, salt, curry powder, cumin, turmeric, and cayenne. Bring to a boil, reduce the heat to low, and simmer until the lentils are soft, about 15 minutes.

2. In a medium skillet over medium heat, heat the olive oil. Add the onion and garlic and sauté until the onion is soft, about 5 minutes. Add the tamari and reduce until the onion is caramelized, about 3 more minutes. Stir the onion mixture and the coconut butter into the cooked lentils.

3. Make the vegetables: Preheat the oven to 400°F. Line a baking sheet with parchment paper.

4. In a medium bowl, toss the yams with 2 tablespoons of the olive oil and 1 teaspoon of the salt, coating the yams well. Spread the yams evenly over the baking sheet and roast for 15 to 20 minutes, until soft, turning once halfway through. Set aside.

5. In a large skillet over medium-high heat, heat the remaining 1 tablespoon olive oil. Add as much of the spinach as will fit, adding more in batches as the spinach wilts, if necessary. Add the remaining 1 teaspoon salt and sauté until the spinach is just wilted, about 3 minutes.

recipe and ingredients continue

3 cups cooked grain of your choice, such as brown rice or quinoa

1 cup Spicy Tomato Jam (page 304)

½ cup Mint-Coconut Chutney (page 305)

2 scallions (white and green parts), chopped

6. To assemble: In a large, shallow serving bowl, spread out the cooked grain as a base and top with a few scoops of the warm lentils. Place the roasted yams on top, followed by the wilted spinach. Drizzle the tomato jam and mint chutney over the bowl and garnish with the chopped scallion.

QUESTION *of the day* / When are you most inspired?

I AM GRATEFUL
Community Bowl

This signature bowl was conceived during the economic downturn of 2008, when a lot of people were really suffering financially. In exchange for a small donation, anyone could come in and enjoy an organic vegan meal, despite their economic situation. As we grew, we decided to charge a minimum fee and donate the proceeds to a nonprofit instead. Despite its philanthropic intentions, though, this bowl continues to be a top seller in the cafés because it's so simple and delicious. It's the perfect meal to prepare at home because of its well-rounded components and inexpensive ingredients.

SERVES 4

4 cups loosely packed chopped kale

3 cups cooked grain of your choice, such as brown rice or quinoa

½ cup Mexican Black Beans (see page 45), or canned

1 cup Garlic Tahini Dressing (page 279)

In a large serving bowl, combine the kale, cooked grains, black beans, and dressing. Toss thoroughly to combine.

I AM EVOLVED
Gratitude Bibimbap Bowl

Like the rest of the world right now, I've become obsessed with Korean food—especially temple cuisine, or dishes that have, for centuries, been produced in Korean, Japanese, and Chinese Buddhist temples. They're traditionally plant-based and are believed to help encourage a calm mind for meditation. While bibimbap isn't necessarily part of the temple food canon, it can be infused with that same beautiful intention. It's warm and satisfying while delivering the quintessential elements of savory, spicy, and crunchy. Here we put our mushroom carnitas to work—this time as mushroom *bulgogi*—along with crispy rice, vegetables, chickpea egg, and a spicy homemade sauce.

SERVES 6

¼ cup plus 1 tablespoon extra-virgin olive oil

4½ cups cooked brown rice or quinoa

1 seedless cucumber, diced

¼ teaspoon Himalayan sea salt

⅛ teaspoon cayenne pepper

Mushroom Carnitas
(see page 175)

Cast-Iron Chickpea Quiche
(page 39)

3 cups shredded romaine lettuce

1½ cups shredded daikon

2 cups Purple Cabbage Kimchi
(page 320)

¾ cup sea palm or wakame, soaked in warm water for 15 minutes and cut into 1-inch pieces

⅓ cup chopped scallions

½ cup bean sprouts

2 cups Adobo Buffalo Sauce
(page 296)

1. Preheat the oven to 400°F.

2. Pour ¼ cup of the olive oil on the hot baking sheet, moving the pan around to distribute the oil evenly across the whole pan. Spread the rice out over the oiled pan and bake for 7 to 10 minutes, until crispy and beginning to brown. Set aside.

3. In a small bowl, combine the cucumber, salt, and cayenne.

4. Heat the remaining 1 tablespoon olive oil in a large skillet over medium-high heat. Add the mushroom carnitas and chickpea egg quiche and sauté until warmed through, about 2 minutes.

5. Divide the crispy rice among 6 individual bowls (soup bowls work well for this). Next to the rice add ½ cup of the romaine to each bowl. Working clockwise, top the rice and lettuce with the shredded daikon, kimchi, seasoned cucumber, and sea palm. Spoon the mushroom carnitas and chickpea egg mixture into the center. Garnish with the scallions and sprouts and serve with the Buffalo sauce on the side.

ENTREÉS

I AM LIBERATED

As an alternative to traditional pastas, we offer a selection of kelp noodle–based dishes. I'm particularly fond of this vehicle because not only are the noodles mild flavored and therefore extremely versatile, but they also deliver the same nutrient- and mineral-dense benefits as other sea vegetables. These are the recipes for our two best-selling variations, but you can prepare the noodles as described here and toss them with anything you'd normally add to pasta.

Basil Hempseed Pesto and Ricotta Kelp Noodles

A lighter, brighter bowl of "pasta."

SERVES 2

For the Kelp Noodles:

One 12-ounce bag kelp noodles (we like Sea Tangle)

½ cup fresh lemon juice

2 teaspoons Himalayan sea salt

To Assemble:

2 cups lightly packed arugula

¼ cup Basil Hempseed Pesto (page 302)

¼ cup Cashew Ricotta (page 311)

¼ cup pitted olives of your choice, halved (we use Kalamata or Italian green olives such as Castelvetrano or Cerignola)

¼ cup cherry tomatoes, halved

2 tablespoons Brazil Nut Parmesan (page 317)

2 teaspoons chopped fresh basil

1. Make the kelp noodles: Cut the kelp noodles into four sections and place them in a colander. Rinse them well with warm water, breaking up the noodles with your hands, and drain.

2. In a large bowl, stir together the lemon juice and salt until the salt has dissolved. Add the noodles and enough hot water to cover. Soak the noodles for 30 minutes, rinse, and drain.

3. Assemble: In a large serving bowl, toss together the noodles, arugula, pesto, and ricotta. Garnish with the olives, tomatoes, Parmesan, and basil and serve.

Pad Thai Kelp Noodles

Takeout comfort food, Café Gratitude–style.

For the Kelp Noodles:

One 12-ounce bag kelp noodles (we like Sea Tangle)

½ cup fresh lemon juice

2 teaspoons Himalayan sea salt

For the Almond Thai Sauce:

½ cup almond butter

½ cup fresh cilantro leaves

½ cup fresh basil leaves

¼ cup fresh lemon juice

¼ jalapeño, seeded

1 tablespoon chopped fresh ginger

1 tablespoon tamari soy sauce

2 teaspoons agave nectar

1 teaspoon Himalayan sea salt

To Assemble:

½ cup shredded carrots

½ cup thinly sliced red bell pepper

½ cup shredded kale

½ cup chopped mixed fresh herbs such as cilantro, basil, and scallions

½ cup sunflower sprouts (optional)

2 tablespoons toasted, chopped almonds

1. Make the kelp noodles: Cut the kelp noodles into four sections and place them in a colander. Rinse them well with warm water, breaking up the noodles with your hands, and drain.

2. In a large bowl, stir together the lemon juice and salt until the salt has dissolved. Add the noodles and enough hot water to cover. Soak the noodles for 30 minutes, rinse, and drain.

3. Make the almond Thai sauce: In a blender, combine the almond butter, cilantro, basil, lemon juice, jalapeño, ginger, tamari, agave nectar, salt, and ¾ cup plus 2 tablespoons water. Blend until smooth.

4. To assemble: In a large serving bowl, toss the noodles with about 1 cup of the sauce, the carrots, pepper, kale, and herbs. Garnish with the sprouts, if using, and toasted almonds.

I AM ELATED
Mole Abuelita Enchiladas

This saucy, cheesy interpretation of the traditional original is a worthy successor to the raw version that used to grace our menu. Thanks to our community of Mexican line cooks, some of the elements here—like our black beans, sweet corn, and mole—are generation-tested family recipes. We then incorporate less customary twists, such as our blackened tempeh and cashew ricotta, for a dish that has made converts of the staunchest of carnivores. I welcome you to play with each of these components to make a dish that's your own, whether it's swapping out the tempeh for mushroom carnitas, layering in some sautéed nopales, or adding in any other Mexican condiment that you enjoy.

SERVES 4

For the Blackened Tempeh:
One 8-ounce block of soybean tempeh

½ small yellow onion, roughly chopped

2 scallions (white and green parts), roughly chopped

1 garlic clove, chopped

1½ tablespoons fresh lime juice

1½ tablespoons tamari soy sauce

1½ tablespoons extra-virgin olive oil, plus more for the pan

1 tablespoon freshly ground black pepper

2 teaspoons coconut sugar

2 teaspoons ground dried thyme

1 teaspoon apple cider vinegar

¾ teaspoon cayenne pepper

½ teaspoon grated fresh ginger

1. Make the blackened tempeh: In a medium pot over high heat, bring 4 cups of water to a boil. Blanch the tempeh in the water for 1 minute and transfer to a medium bowl or baking dish. Set aside to cool while you make the marinade.

2. In a blender or food processor, combine the onion, scallions, garlic, lime juice, tamari, olive oil, 2 teaspoons of the black pepper, the coconut sugar, 1 teaspoon of the thyme, the apple cider vinegar, ¼ teaspoon of the cayenne, the ginger, jalapeño, allspice, and nutmeg and blend until smooth.

3. Pour the marinade over the tempeh, cover, and refrigerate overnight or up to 12 hours.

4. On a large plate, combine the remaining 1 teaspoon black pepper, the remaining 1 teaspoon thyme, the remaining ½ teaspoon cayenne, the paprika, chipotle powder, oregano, and smoked salt. Remove the tempeh from the marinade and shake off any excess. Coat the block of tempeh in the blackening spices.

recipe and ingredients continue

½ teaspoon seeded and chopped jalapeño

½ teaspoon ground allspice

⅛ teaspoon ground nutmeg

3 tablespoons paprika

1 teaspoon chipotle powder

1 teaspoon dried oregano

½ teaspoon smoked sea salt

To Assemble:

2 tablespoons extra-virgin olive oil

1 recipe Black Mole Abuelita (page 285)

2 cups fresh or frozen and thawed corn kernels

½ teaspoon seeded and chopped jalapeño

¼ teaspoon Himalayan sea salt

8 corn tortillas

1 cup Mexican Black Beans (see page 45)

2 avocados, cubed

1 cup Roasted Tomatillo Sauce (page 295)

Cashew Ricotta (page 311)

2 tablespoons chopped fresh cilantro

1 teaspoon sesame seeds

1 recipe Creamy Mexican Coleslaw (see page 175)

2 cups Escabeche (page 319)

5. In a medium skillet over medium-high heat, heat enough olive oil to coat the bottom of the pan. Lay the tempeh in the pan and blacken on each side, about 3 minutes per side. Add more oil if the pan starts to look dry. Remove the tempeh and set aside to cool. When the tempeh is cool enough to handle, cut it into ½-inch cubes.

6. Assemble the enchiladas: In a large skillet over medium-high heat, heat 1 tablespoon of the olive oil. Add the cubed tempeh and 2 cups of the mole abuelita and cook until warmed through. Remove the pan from the heat.

7. In a medium skillet over medium-high heat, heat the remaining 1 tablespoon of olive oil. Add the corn, jalapeño, and salt and sauté until the corn begins to soften and caramelize, about 5 minutes. Transfer the corn to a bowl and set aside.

8. Wipe the skillet clean and heat over high heat. Warm the tortillas until they take on a bit of char, about 1 minute per side. If you have a gas stove, you could also do this directly over the flame. Stack the tortillas under a clean kitchen towel to keep them warm and pliable.

9. Fill each tortilla with a spoonful of black beans, a spoonful of corn, a few cubes of the tempeh, and a few pieces of avocado. (Reserve the extra mole sauce in the pan for topping the enchiladas later.) Roll up the tortillas and arrange them on a platter, seam-side down. Tuck the enchiladas closely next to one another as you go, to help keep them rolled.

10. Top the enchiladas with the roasted tomatillo sauce and the remaining mole. Drizzle cashew ricotta over the top and scatter with the cilantro and sesame seeds. Serve with Mexican coleslaw and escabeche.

NOTE You will want to leave time to marinate the tempeh for 12 hours.

I AM DYNAMIC
Baked Garnet Yam and Cauliflower Samosa Chaat with Chana Masala, Mint-Coconut Chutney, and Spicy Tomato Jam

Our take on the classic Indian samosa is both traditional and unconventional at the same time. I wanted to keep the dish on the lighter side by baking the samosas instead of frying them, and use a flaky herbed whole-wheat crust instead of the usual samosa pastry. Otherwise we stay pretty true to the original here, toasting and blending our own spices for the Bengali garam masala and the classic chana masala spice blends. You can buy a variety of quality Indian spice blends, but toasting your own whole seeds and grinding them is so easy to do and really makes the flavors shine that much brighter. Feel free to use the leftover Bengali garam masala in place of store-bought blends for anything else you might cook at home.

SERVES 4

For the Bengali Garam Masala Powder:

2½ teaspoons sesame seeds

1½ teaspoons whole green peppercorns

1½ teaspoons whole black peppercorns

1½ teaspoons whole white peppercorns

1 teaspoon whole cloves

5 green cardamom pods (interior black seeds only)

1 tablespoon cumin seeds

3 tablespoons coriander seeds

1 dried bay leaf

1. Make the Bengali garam masala powder: In a large saucepan over low heat, combine the sesame seeds, peppercorns, cloves, cardamom pods, cumin seeds, coriander seeds, and bay leaf. Toast until fragrant. Allow the spices to cool before grinding in a spice or coffee grinder. Transfer the mixture to a small bowl and stir in the ginger and cayenne. Reserve 1 teaspoon for the samosa filling and store the rest, tightly covered, in a jar for up to 6 months.

2. Make the samosa dough: Whenever you are making a pastry crust, you will want to keep all of your ingredients as cold as possible while working, to keep the fat from blending too completely with the flour, which will make the crust less than flaky.

recipe and ingredients continue

¼ teaspoon ginger powder

1 teaspoon cayenne pepper

For the Samosa Dough:

1¾ cups unbleached all-purpose flour

2 cups whole-wheat flour

2 teaspoons baking powder

1½ teaspoons Himalayan sea salt

1½ cups coconut oil, plus more, melted, for brushing the finished samosas

¼ cup finely chopped fresh cilantro

¼ cup finely chopped fresh basil

2 scallions (white and green parts), finely chopped

1 tablespoon apple cider vinegar

¾ cup ice water, or as needed

For the Samosa Filling:

3 cups cauliflower florets (roughly 1-inch each)

2 cups 1-inch pieces garnet yams

¼ cup plus 2 tablespoons extra-virgin olive oil

1 teaspoon Himalayan sea salt, plus more to taste

1 tablespoon grated or finely chopped fresh ginger

1 small jalapeño, seeded and finely chopped

1 teaspoon yellow mustard seeds

2 Roma tomatoes, diced

1½ teaspoons coriander seeds

½ teaspoon turmeric powder

1 teaspoon Bengali Garam Masala Powder (above) or store-bought

1 cup finely chopped kale

2 tablespoons chopped fresh cilantro

3. In a large bowl, combine the all-purpose flour, whole-wheat flour, baking powder, and salt and mix gently to combine. Set the bowl in the refrigerator or freezer for 30 minutes to chill.

4. Scoop the coconut oil onto a small plate or into a bowl and set it in the refrigerator until it solidifies, about 10 minutes. Once it's hard, quickly cut it into small pieces.

5. In a food processor, combine the flour mixture, cilantro, basil, scallions, and coconut oil. Pulse just until the mixture is crumbly. Do not overmix.

6. Add the apple cider vinegar and half of the ice water and pulse until the dough comes together. Continue to add water to the dough until the dough is smooth and pliable. You may not need to add all of it. Turn out the dough onto a sheet of plastic wrap, quickly press it into a disc shape, and wrap it tightly. Let the dough chill in the refrigerator for at least 10 minutes before portioning it, or up to 3 days if making ahead.

7. Make the samosa filling: Preheat the oven to 375°F.

8. In a large bowl, toss the cauliflower and yams with ¼ cup of the olive oil and the salt. Spread the mixture over a baking sheet in a single layer and roast for 20 to 30 minutes. Check the vegetables after 15 minutes to turn them over so they cook evenly, and continue checking every 10 minutes or so, giving them a turn, until you can pierce them easily with a fork. Set aside.

9. Heat the remaining 2 tablespoons of olive oil in a large, heavy-bottomed skillet over medium heat. Add the ginger, jalapeño, and mustard seeds and cook the mixture briefly until the mustard seeds begin to pop, about 30 seconds. Add the tomatoes, coriander, turmeric, and garam masala. Allow the tomatoes to cook for 5 to 7 minutes, until they begin to break down and the mixture begins to thicken. Stir in the roasted cauliflower and the yams. Turn them over

recipe and ingredients continue

2 tablespoons chopped
fresh basil

2 tablespoons chopped scallions
(white and green parts)

1 tablespoon fresh lemon juice

For the Chana Masala:
One 2-inch cinnamon stick

2 tablespoons coriander seeds

1 tablespoon fennel seeds

1 tablespoon cumin seeds

1 whole dried chipotle pepper

½ teaspoon whole cloves

2 green cardamom pods

¼ teaspoon whole black
peppercorns

2 cups unsweetened shredded
coconut flakes

½ cup extra-virgin olive oil

½ cup coconut oil

2 teaspoons yellow mustard
seeds

1 cup chopped red onion

1½ teaspoons finely chopped
garlic

1½ teaspoons finely chopped
fresh ginger

1 tablespoon seeded and
chopped jalapeño

1 cup diced fresh tomatoes

8 cups cooked chickpeas
(homemade or canned, no-
salt-added beans, drained and
rinsed)

1 dried curry leaf

¼ teaspoon turmeric powder

2 teaspoons Himalayan sea salt

For Serving:
Spicy Tomato Jam (page 304)

Mint-Coconut Chutney
(page 305)

in the tomato sauté until they are well coated and warmed through, about 5 minutes.

10. Add the kale, cilantro, basil, scallions, and lemon juice, and cook for an additional minute or 2 to bring the flavors together. If the pan gets dry, add 1 to 2 tablespoons of water. Taste and adjust for salt. The mixture should neither be too wet nor too dry and should hold together when pressed. Set the mixture aside and let it cool until you are ready to make the samosas.

11. Make the chana masala: In a large skillet over medium heat, toast the cinnamon stick, coriander seeds, fennel seeds, cumin seeds, chipotle, cloves, cardamom pods, and black peppercorns until everything is warm and fragrant, about 3 minutes. Add the shredded coconut and continue to toast until the coconut shreds are dark golden in color, 3 to 5 more minutes.

12. Remove the black inner seeds from the cardamom pods and discard the outer green shell. In a blender, combine the coconut spice mixture, the black cardamom seeds, and 1½ cups of water and blend the mixture into a smooth paste. If necessary, add an extra tablespoon or 2 of water to loosen the paste.

13. In a large pot over medium heat, heat the olive and coconut oils for 1 minute. Add the mustard seeds and cook for another minute, or until the seeds begin to pop. Be careful not to burn them! Add the onion, garlic, ginger, and jalapeño and cook for 2 minutes or until the onion is translucent. Add the tomatoes, chickpeas, curry leaf, turmeric, and salt plus 2 cups of water. Partially cover the pot and cook for 10 minutes until the tomatoes have begun to break down. Add more water, as needed, if the mixture becomes too dry.

14. Add the coconut spice puree to the pot and cook for 5 to 7 minutes, until the pot reaches a light boil. Reduce the heat to low, partially cover the pot, and simmer for an additional 10 minutes, or until the chickpeas are soft and flavorful and

NOTE Each of these components can be made up to a few days in advance, including the assembled samosas, which you can freeze and pull out when you're ready to bake them (just add about 10 minutes to the baking time). If you're looking for a satisfying appetizer, you can skip the chana masala and just serve the samosas with the spicy tomato jam and mint-coconut chutney.

the broth is reduced to the consistency of a thick cream. Discard the curry leaf. Keep warm until ready to serve.

15. Make the samosas: Preheat the oven to 400°F. Line a large baking sheet with parchment paper or a silicone baking mat and set aside.

16. You can roll out your dough traditionally with a rolling pin on a floured surface or you can use our nontraditional Gratitude method of using a tortilla press to make the pastry discs for your samosas.

17. Portion the dough into 12 even pieces. If you are rolling them out, lightly flour your work surface and roll out the dough to a 6-inch circle that is approximately ⅛ inch thick.

18. If you are using a tortilla press, simply press the dough between 2 sheets of parchment paper cut to the size of your tortilla press until you have a disc the same dimensions as above. You can reuse the parchment paper a number of times before it will become too moist.

19. As you work, keep the discs in a cool spot so they don't become too soft to manage.

20. When all of the discs are ready, fill the center of each with ⅓ cup of the samosa filling. Dip your index finger in water and line the edges of the dough with a bit of water to help seal the samosas. Bring the edges of the dough around the filling, pinching them together in a 3-pointed star. This is not the traditional samosa shape, but it is really pretty and works well with our light and flaky samosa pastry dough.

21. Transfer the samosas to the baking sheet and brush each samosa with a little melted coconut oil. Bake for 25 to 30 minutes, until they are golden brown.

22. Serve: Transfer the warm chana masala to a serving plate and place the hot samosas on top. At the cafés, we plate this dish with the spicy tomato jam and mint-coconut chutney drizzled over the top of the samosas, but you could serve them on the side and allow everyone to dip as they please.

I AM FEARLESS
Meatballs in Marinara with Arugula and Cashew Crème Fraiche

It's not hard to guess that this dish was inspired by the tried-and-true Italian meatballs in marinara. We lightened up our version with some fresh arugula so you can get your greens in and, of course, by making our meatballs completely plant-based, with beets to give them their signature reddish color, as well as mushrooms to deepen their flavor. You could also reinterpret this dish as an appetizer (as we originally did) by skewering the baked meatballs and serving them with marinara sauce for dipping.

SERVES 4

1 cup balsamic vinegar (or golden balsamic for a more amber color)

¼ cup coconut nectar

1 head radicchio

2 tablespoons extra-virgin olive oil, plus more for drizzling

½ teaspoon Himalayan sea salt

¼ teaspoon freshly ground black pepper

Blackened Tempeh Meatballs (see page 109)

2½ cups Marinara Sauce (page 212)

1 cup baby arugula

Cashew Crème Fraiche (page 315)

Red chili flakes (optional)

Brazil Nut Parmesan (page 317)

1. In a small pot over high heat, combine the balsamic vinegar and coconut nectar. Bring to a boil and reduce the heat to low. Simmer until the mixture has reduced to ½ cup, 20 to 30 minutes. Set aside to cool. The reduction will thicken a bit more as it cools.

2. Preheat a grill, grill pan, or cast-iron skillet over high heat.

3. Separate the leaves from the radicchio and place them in a large bowl. Massage the olive oil into the radicchio and sprinkle with the salt and pepper. When the grill or pan is hot, char the radicchio leaves until wilted and tender, turning often, about 5 minutes. Lay the grilled radicchio on a serving platter or in a serving bowl.

4. In a large skillet or pot over medium-high heat, combine the meatballs and marinara and cook until just heated through, about 5 minutes. Pour the warmed meatballs and marinara over the grilled radicchio leaves. Scatter the arugula over the meatballs and drizzle with the cashew ricotta, some olive oil, and the balsamic reduction. Sprinkle with the red chili flakes, if using, and garnish with the Brazil nut Parmesan.

I AM FABULOUS

Mexican-Style Raw Lasagna with Sweet Corn, Raw Cacao Mole, and Pumpkin Seed Pesto

Whether you consider this a lasagna or a generous composed summer salad (technically both are true!), this is a fresh, bright, and slightly surprising entrée. The zucchini noodles lend themselves to pretty much any flavor profile, but our most popular version of this dish is undoubtedly this Mexican-inspired version. We layer the noodles with deeply flavored cacao mole, herbaceous pesto, sweet corn and tomatoes, and squash blossoms when they're in season, and the result is a meal that is quite substantial but won't leave you feeling weighed down.

SERVES 8

5 small zucchini or summer squash

Himalayan sea salt, to taste

¼ cup Cilantro Pumpkin Seed Pesto (page 301)

¼ cup extra-virgin olive oil

4 cups packed baby spinach

1¼ cups Cashew Ricotta (page 311)

1½ cups Raw Cacao Mole (page 288)

4 cups cherry tomatoes, halved

4 cups fresh sweet corn kernels or frozen, thawed

20 squash blossoms, stems trimmed (optional)

1. Using a vegetable peeler or mandoline, thinly slice the squash lengthwise into noodles. You should have about 6 cups of noodles. Lay the noodles in a colander, sprinkle them with a generous pinch of salt, and toss to coat. Let them sit over a sink or bowl for at least 30 minutes or up to 1 hour, allowing any excess liquid to drain. Lay the squash noodles out on a few layers of paper towels and blot dry.

2. In a small bowl, whisk together the pesto and olive oil.

3. In a large baking dish (9-inch x 13-inch or larger), layer about a third of the zucchini noodles, half of the spinach, half of the ricotta, ½ cup of the mole, half of the tomatoes, half of the corn, a third of the squash blossoms, if using, and half of the pesto-oil mixture.

4. Repeat with another layer, reserving a third each of the zucchini noodles, mole, and squash blossoms.

5. To top the lasagna, lay down the last of the zucchini noodles, spread the remaining mole, and arrange the remaining squash blossoms on top. Slice and serve.

I AM GIVING
Ancient Grain Pizzas

Everybody loves pizza, which is why we knew that we had to include a selection of them on our menu. Where we've tried to go with it is to use the crust to showcase alternative grains that are either California heirlooms or products of sustainable, regenerative agriculture. When we don't have access to those, we look to original wheat grains that haven't been hybridized, like Kamut and einkorn. Otherwise, it's a super-simple dough that becomes a great palette for the toppings to shine. Our mozzarella and ricotta cheeses in particular will keep you from missing traditional pies because they cook so well.

Ancient Grain Pizza Dough

**MAKES THREE
10-INCH PIZZAS**

3¼ teaspoons active dry yeast

1 teaspoon cane sugar

1¼ cups Kamut flour, plus more for dusting

1 cup plus 1 tablespoon einkorn flour

½ teaspoon Himalayan sea salt

1 teaspoon extra-virgin olive oil

1. In a medium bowl, combine the yeast and sugar with ⅔ cup of warm water. Mix gently to dissolve the sugar and set in a warm place to proof until bubbly, 10 to 15 minutes.

2. In the bowl of a stand mixer fitted with the hook attachment, combine the Kamut flour, einkorn flour, and salt. Add the yeast mixture and an additional 1¼ cups of warm water and mix on low speed until the dough is smooth and elastic, 3 to 5 minutes.

3. Turn the dough out onto a floured surface and knead it with your hands into a tight round. Return the dough to the bowl, drizzle it with the olive oil, and use your hands to spread the oil over the exposed surface of the dough. Cover the bowl with a clean towel and set in a warm place for 1½ to 2 hours, until doubled in size.

4. Punch down the dough and portion it into roughly equal thirds (220 grams each, if you're using a kitchen scale). The dough can be used immediately, refrigerated in a covered container for up to 8 hours, or frozen in a sealed baggie for up to 1 month.

Marinara Sauce

MAKES 2 QUARTS

¼ cup extra-virgin olive oil

2 tablespoons chopped garlic

4½ pounds fresh tomatoes, chopped

1½ teaspoons Himalayan sea salt

1½ teaspoons smoked salt

⅓ cup packed fresh basil leaves, chopped

2 teaspoons sugar

1. In a large sauté pan over medium heat, heat the olive oil. Add the garlic and cook until just golden, about 1 minute. Add the tomatoes, sea salt, and smoked salt and cook, stirring frequently, for 20 to 30 minutes, until the tomatoes have cooked down and the sauce has thickened.

2. Remove from the heat and stir in the basil and sugar. Let the residual heat of the sauce dissolve the sugar as you stir, about 1 minute. Use right away or store covered in the refrigerator for up to 1 week. (This also freezes beautifully.)

Hawaiian Pizza

MAKES ONE 10-INCH PIZZA

Whole-grain or all-purpose flour of choice, for dusting

1 ball Ancient Grain Pizza Dough (page 211)

2 teaspoons extra-virgin olive oil

¼ cup Marinara Sauce (above)

⅓ cup chopped fresh pineapple

¼ cup crumbled Blackened Tempeh (see page 199)

2 tablespoons Barbecue Sauce (page 307)

2 tablespoons crumbled Cashew Mozzarella (page 312)

¼ cup plus 2 tablespoons Cashew Ricotta (page 311)

⅛ teaspoon chipotle powder

¼ cup Coconut Bacon (see page 102)

1 tablespoon Brazil Nut Parmesan (page 317)

1 tablespoon chopped fresh cilantro

1. Preheat the oven to 450°F. If you're using a pizza stone or steel, place it in the oven to preheat. Line a round pizza pan, baking sheet, or pizza peel with parchment paper.

2. On a floured work surface, stretch or roll out the pizza dough to a 10-inch round. Place the dough on the parchment paper. Drizzle or brush 1 teaspoon of the olive oil over the dough. Top with the marinara, using a spoon to spread it around to about 1 inch from the edge. Scatter the pineapple over the top of the pizza, followed by the blackened tempeh, barbecue sauce, mozzarella, and ¼ cup of the ricotta. Sprinkle the chipotle powder on top and drizzle with the remaining teaspoon of olive oil.

3. Bake for 10 to 15 minutes, until the crust is crisp and the cheeses have softened. Garnish with the remaining 2 tablespoons ricotta, the coconut bacon, Parmesan, and cilantro. Serve hot.

Braised Mushroom Pizza

For the Braised Mushrooms:
1 teaspoon extra-virgin olive oil
1 small garlic clove, chopped
1 cup sliced shiitake mushrooms
⅛ teaspoon Himalayan sea salt
1 teaspoon white wine

To Assemble:
Brown rice flour or all-purpose flour of choice, for dusting
1 ball Ancient Grain Pizza Dough (page 211)
2 teaspoons extra-virgin olive oil
¼ cup Marinara Sauce (page 212)
2 tablespoons crumbled Cashew Mozzarella (page 312)
¼ cup plus 2 tablespoons Cashew Ricotta (page 311)
1 tablespoon Brazil Nut Parmesan (page 317)
4 fresh basil leaves, torn or chopped

1. Make the braised mushrooms: Heat the olive oil in a medium skillet over medium-high heat. Add the garlic and cook until just fragrant and beginning to turn golden, about 1 minute. Add the mushrooms and cook for 2 to 3 minutes, until they've released their water. Sprinkle in the salt and continue cooking for another 3 minutes. Pour in the white wine and allow the alcohol to evaporate, about 2 minutes. Remove the pan from the heat and set aside.

2. Assemble the pizza: Preheat the oven to 450°F. If you're using a pizza stone or steel, place it in the oven to preheat. Line a round pizza pan, baking sheet, or pizza peel with parchment paper.

3. On a floured work surface, stretch or roll out the pizza dough to a 10-inch round. Place the dough on the parchment paper. Drizzle or brush 1 teaspoon of the olive oil over the dough. Top with the marinara, using a spoon to spread it around to about 1 inch from the edge. Scatter the mushrooms over the top, followed by the mozzarella and ¼ cup of the ricotta. Drizzle with the remaining teaspoon of olive oil.

4. Bake for 10 to 15 minutes, until the crust is crisp and the cheeses have softened. Garnish with the remaining 2 tablespoons ricotta, the Parmesan, and basil.

Braised Asparagus Pizza

MAKES ONE 10-INCH
PIZZA

For the Braised Asparagus:

2 teaspoons extra-virgin
olive oil

¼ cup chopped yellow onion

1 bunch asparagus, ends
trimmed, cut into 1-inch lengths,
tops left whole

½ teaspoon Himalayan sea salt

1 tablespoon chopped fresh
parsley

1 tablespoon chopped fresh
mint

¼ teaspoon freshly ground
black pepper

To Assemble:

Brown rice flour or all-purpose
flour of choice, for dusting

1 ball Ancient Grain Pizza
Dough (page 211)

2 teaspoons extra-virgin
olive oil

¼ cup Marinara Sauce
(page 212)

2 tablespoons crumbled
Cashew Mozzarella
(page 312)

¼ cup plus 2 tablespoons
Cashew Ricotta (page 311)

1 tablespoon Brazil Nut
Parmesan (page 317)

1 tablespoon Gremolata
(page 293)

1. Make the braised asparagus: Heat the olive oil in a large skillet over medium-high heat. Add the onion and cook for 3 to 4 minutes, until the onion has softened. Add the asparagus and salt and continue sautéing for 3 minutes. Add ¼ cup of water, cover the pan, and cook for 8 to 10 minutes, until the asparagus is tender. Stir in the parsley, mint, and pepper and remove the pan from the heat.

2. Assemble the pizza: Preheat the oven to 450°F. If you're using a pizza stone or steel, place it in the oven to preheat. Line a round pizza pan, baking sheet, or pizza peel with parchment paper.

3. On a floured work surface, stretch or roll out the pizza dough to a 10-inch round. Place the dough on the parchment paper. Drizzle or brush 1 teaspoon of the olive oil over the dough. Top with the marinara, using a spoon to spread it around to about 1 inch from the edge. Scatter the braised asparagus over the top, followed by the mozzarella and ¼ cup of the ricotta. Drizzle with the remaining teaspoon of olive oil.

4. Bake for 10 to 15 minutes, until the crust is crisp and the cheeses have softened. Garnish with the remaining ricotta, Parmesan, and gremolata. Serve hot.

Margherita Pizza

MAKES ONE 10-INCH PIZZA

Whole-grain or all-purpose flour of choice, for dusting

1 ball Ancient Grain Pizza Dough (page 211)

2 teaspoons extra-virgin olive oil

¼ cup Marinara Sauce (page 212)

1 tablespoon Basil Hempseed Pesto (page 302) or Sun-dried Tomato Pesto (page 303)

6 to 8 cherry tomatoes, halved

2 tablespoons crumbled Cashew Mozzarella (page 312)

2 tablespoons Cashew Ricotta (page 311)

1 tablespoon Brazil Nut Parmesan (page 317)

4 fresh basil leaves, chopped or torn

¼ teaspoon smoked sea salt

1. Preheat the oven to 450°F. If you're using a pizza stone or steel, place it in the oven to preheat. Line a round pizza pan, baking sheet, or pizza peel with parchment paper.

2. On a floured work surface, stretch or roll out the pizza dough to a 10-inch round. Place the dough on the parchment paper. Drizzle or brush 1 teaspoon of the olive oil over the dough. Top with the marinara, using a spoon to spread it around to about 1 inch from the edge. Add the pesto in small dollops and top with the cherry tomatoes and cashew mozzarella. Drizzle with the remaining 1 teaspoon olive oil.

3. Bake for 10 to 15 minutes, until the crust is crisp and the cheese has softened. Garnish with the ricotta, Parmesan, and basil, and finish with a sprinkle of smoked salt. Serve hot.

I AM DEVOTED
Gratitude Blue Plate Special with Lentil–Garnet Yam Meatloaf, Mashed Potatoes with Shiitake Gravy, Slaw, and Pickled Beets

Of all the dishes I've come up with for our menu, I think this one was the most fun. I wanted to work off of the idea of the blue plate special—traditionally a protein with three vegetable sides, one of which is usually mashed potatoes and gravy. I got to thinking about old-school American classics and landed on meatloaf, which we've reimagined with lentils and yams. Then we updated all the fixin's—coleslaw, greens, pickled beets—and have been serving this very popular dish ever since.

SERVES 6

For the French Lentil and Garnet Yam Loaves:

1 large garnet yam or sweet potato, peeled and cut into ½-inch cubes

3 tablespoons extra-virgin olive oil, plus more for the pans

1 tablespoon chopped fresh rosemary

1½ teaspoons Himalayan sea salt

¼ teaspoon freshly ground black pepper

1 cup walnuts, toasted

¼ cup pumpkin seeds

½ cup chopped red onion

2 tablespoons thinly sliced celery

1 teaspoon chopped garlic

2 tablespoons white wine

1 tablespoon finely chopped fresh parsley

1. Make the French lentil and garnet yam loaves: Preheat the oven to 400°F. Line a baking sheet with parchment paper.

2. In a medium bowl, toss the cubed sweet potato with 1 tablespoon of the olive oil, the rosemary, ½ teaspoon of the salt, and the pepper. Spread the cubes onto the baking sheet and roast for 20 minutes or until soft and beginning to brown on the edges, shaking the pan once halfway through to ensure even cooking. Remove from the oven and set aside.

3. Reduce the oven temperature to 350°F and grease 6 mini loaf pans or muffin cups with a small amount of olive oil.

4. In a food processor, combine the walnuts and pumpkin seeds and process until the mixture is fine and crumbly. Set aside.

5. In a large skillet over medium heat, heat the remaining 2 tablespoons of olive oil. Add the onion, celery, and garlic and sauté until the onion and celery have softened, about 5 minutes. Add the white wine and parsley and stir for a minute until the alcohol cooks off.

recipe and ingredients continue

2 cups cooked French lentils (from 1 scant cup dried lentils)

1 cup butternut squash puree (you can steam and puree your own or use canned)

½ cup shredded carrots

½ cup grated apple

1 teaspoon smoked salt

½ cup diced fresh tomato

For the Butternut Squash and Shiitake Gravy:

2 tablespoons extra-virgin olive oil

2 teaspoons chopped garlic

½ cup thinly sliced celery

½ pound shiitake mushrooms, stemmed and roughly chopped

2 tablespoons chopped fresh thyme and/or rosemary

½ cup white wine

1½ teaspoons smoked salt

¼ teaspoon freshly ground black pepper

2 cups butternut squash puree (you can steam and puree your own or use canned)

3 dried bay leaves

1 teaspoon Himalayan sea salt

For the Smashed Heirloom Potatoes:

2½ pounds small heirloom-variety potatoes (about 8 cups)

1 teaspoon Himalayan sea salt

4 cups Coconut Milk (page 32) or store-bought

½ cup Brazil Nut Parmesan (page 317)

3 tablespoons extra-virgin olive oil

1 teaspoon smoked salt

1 teaspoon chopped garlic

6. Add the roasted sweet potatoes and walnut–pumpkin seed mixture, along with the lentils, ½ cup of the squash, carrots, apple, smoked salt, and the remaining teaspoon of Himalayan sea salt. Stir and turn the mixture thoroughly so all of the ingredients are fully combined.

7. Divide the mixture among the 6 mini loaf pans or muffin wells. Top the loaves with a generous tablespoon each of the diced tomato and the remaining butternut squash puree. Bake for 30 minutes, or until the loaves are browned and firm on top.

8. Make the butternut squash and shiitake gravy: In a large, wide saucepan over medium heat, heat the olive oil. Add the garlic and celery and sauté for 3 minutes, until the celery has softened. Add the mushrooms and herbs and cook for 10 minutes, stirring frequently, until the mushrooms have given up most, if not all, of their water.

9. Add the white wine, ½ teaspoon of the smoked salt, and the pepper. Cook for another 5 minutes. Add 2½ cups of water, the squash puree, bay leaves, sea salt, and the remaining teaspoon of smoked salt. Reduce the heat to low and gently simmer for 10 to 15 minutes, until the mixture is uniform and slightly reduced.

10. Remove and discard the bay leaves and use an immersion blender to puree the mixture into a smooth gravy. Alternatively, you can use a blender, being careful with the hot liquid.

11. Make the smashed heirloom potatoes: In a large pot over medium-high heat, cover the potatoes with water by about an inch. Bring to a boil and add the salt. Reduce the heat to medium to keep the potatoes at a low boil and cook until the potatoes are soft, about 15 minutes. Drain the potatoes and place them back in the warm pot, covered, to keep warm.

12. In a medium pot over medium-high heat, heat the coconut milk for 5 minutes, until warm and uniform in texture.

For the Garlicky Greens:

2 tablespoons extra-virgin olive oil

2 teaspoons chopped garlic

12 cups lightly packed chopped fresh kale, chard, or collard greens

2 tablespoons white wine

¾ teaspoon Himalayan sea salt

For Serving:

¼ cup Brazil Nut Parmesan (page 317)

1½ cups Creamy Mexican Coleslaw (see page 175)

Pickled Beets (page 322)

3 scallions (white and green parts), chopped

13. In a large bowl, combine the warm potatoes, coconut milk, Brazil nut parmesan, olive oil, smoked salt, and garlic. Smash the potatoes with a potato masher until everything is blended and creamy, but the potatoes maintain some shape and chunky texture.

14. Make the garlicky greens: In a large pot or large, wide saucepan over medium-high heat, heat the olive oil. Add the garlic and sauté until just golden, about 30 seconds. Add as many of the greens as will fit, working in batches as they wilt if necessary. Cook the greens for 5 minutes, until wilted but still bright green. Add the white wine and the salt and cook for another 2 minutes, just until the alcohol has dissipated.

15. Serve: On individual dinner plates, place 1 lentil squash loaf and a scoop of the smashed potatoes. Spoon the gravy over the potatoes and sprinkle with the Parmesan. Nestle some of the greens next to the loaf, along with some of the coleslaw. Garnish with a few wedges of pickled beets and the chopped scallions.

I AM WELCOMING
Mediterranean Plate with Falafel, Eggplant Salad, and Hempseed Tabbouleh

Since we didn't exactly go traditional with this sampler, let's just call it a Mediterranean-*inspired* assortment. It's essentially a blend of spices and textures that you'd traditionally find in Middle Eastern and North African cuisines (and, in the case of the tomato jam, Indian). But it all comes together as a beautiful whole, perhaps made more so by the mishmash of cultural connections.

SERVES 4

For the Harissa:
4 dried whole guajillo chilies
2 dried whole chipotle chilies
1 sun-dried tomato
1 teaspoon coriander seeds
1 teaspoon cumin seeds
1 teaspoon caraway seeds
1 medium red bell pepper
¼ cup extra-virgin olive oil
¾ cup diced red onion
1 tablespoon chopped garlic
1 teaspoon lemon zest
½ teaspoon smoked salt, plus more to taste

For the Hempseed Tabbouleh:
2 tablespoons fresh lemon juice
1½ tablespoons extra-virgin olive oil
1 teaspoon chopped garlic
½ teaspoon Himalayan sea salt
2½ cups finely chopped fresh parsley
1½ cups diced cucumber

1. Make the harissa: In a medium bowl, soak the dried chilies and sun-dried tomato in hot water for 15 minutes, until softened. Drain and reserve 1 cup of the soaking water. Chop the chilies and set aside in a small bowl. Set aside the tomato.

2. In a small skillet over medium heat, add the coriander, cumin, and caraway seeds and toast until just fragrant. Set aside to cool.

3. If you have a gas range, turn the flame to medium heat. Using a pair of metal tongs, carefully roast the red pepper over the open flame until it is black and starting to blister all the way around. Alternatively, you can roast the pepper on a sheet pan under the broiler, turning the pepper every minute or so until it is blackened. Wrap the pepper in parchment paper and set it aside to cool. When the pepper is cool enough to handle, slip off the skin over a bowl or sink. Slice open the pepper and remove the stem and seeds. Set the roasted pepper aside.

4. In a large skillet over medium heat, heat 2 tablespoons of the olive oil. Add the red onion, garlic, and chopped chilies. Cover and cook, stirring occasionally, until well caramelized, about 5 minutes. Add a little of the soaking water from the chilies if the mixture seems too dry.

recipe and ingredients continue

1½ cups diced fresh tomatoes

¼ cup hempseeds

3 tablespoons diced red onion

For the Falafels:

1¼ cups dried chickpeas, soaked overnight, drained, and rinsed

½ cup chopped red onion

¼ cup chopped fresh parsley

¼ cup chopped fresh cilantro

Zest of 1 lemon

2 teaspoons chopped garlic

2 tablespoons garbanzo flour or other gluten-free flour of choice

1 teaspoon baking powder

1 teaspoon Himalayan sea salt

½ teaspoon ground cumin

½ teaspoon ground coriander

¼ teaspoon ground cardamom

¼ teaspoon cayenne pepper

Frying oil of choice (rice bran oil or sunflower oil works well)

1 cup white sesame seeds

For Serving:

Pita or gluten-free bread of choice

Extra-virgin olive oil, for grilling and drizzling

1 cup Eggplant Caponata (page 94)

1 seedless cucumber, sliced

¼ teaspoon Himalayan sea salt

½ cup Spicy Tomato Jam (page 304)

1½ cups Raw Zucchini Cilantro Hummus (page 298)

1 cup pitted Kalamata olives

3 tablespoons Gremolata (page 293)

5. In a blender or food processor, combine the onion-chili mixture, toasted spices, roasted red pepper, sun-dried tomato, the remaining 2 tablespoons olive oil, lemon zest, smoked salt, and ½ cup of the chili soaking water. Blend until the mixture is smooth. Taste and adjust for salt if needed.

6. Make the hempseed tabbouleh: In a medium bowl, whisk together the lemon juice, olive oil, garlic, and salt. Add the parsley, cucumber, tomatoes, hempseeds, and onion and toss to combine. Refrigerate while you make the falafel.

7. Make the falafels: In a food processor, combine the soaked chickpeas, onion, parsley, cilantro, lemon zest, and garlic. Process until everything is finely chopped but not yet a paste. The mixture should hold together when pressed with a spoon or spatula.

8. In a large bowl, combine the chickpea mixture, garbanzo flour, baking powder, salt, cumin, coriander, cardamom, and cayenne and mix thoroughly to combine. Refrigerate the mixture for at least 1 hour.

9. In a deep, heavy-bottomed pot or high-sided skillet over medium-high heat, add 2 inches' worth of oil and heat to 350°F. Line a plate with paper towels and set it near the stove.

10. While the oil heats, use a ¼-cup measure to portion the chickpea mixture into small patties. Use your hands to press each falafel into a ball, then flatten slightly into an oblong shape. Sprinkle both sides with sesame seeds.

11. Working in small batches, carefully and gently lay the falafels into the hot oil and fry for about 3 minutes per side, until deeply golden brown and crisp. Adjust the heat on the burner as you go to make sure the oil doesn't get too hot or too cool, and bring the temperature of the oil back to 350°F in between batches. Remove the fried falafels to the paper towel–lined plate to drain and cool slightly.

12. Serve: Preheat a grill, grill pan, or large skillet over medium-high heat.

13. Brush the pitas or bread of choice with a small amount of olive oil and grill until warmed and slightly crisp, 1 to 2 minutes per side.

14. In a small pot over medium heat, warm the caponata.

15. In a small bowl, toss the cucumber slices with the salt.

16. On a large serving platter, arrange the components in small groupings: the falafels, tabbouleh, grilled pita or bread, caponata, salted cucumber slices, tomato jam, zucchini hummus, and olives. Drizzle a few tablespoons of olive oil over the hummus and as desired over the rest of the platter. Garnish with the harissa and a dusting of gremolata.

QUESTION *of the day* / What moves you to tears?

I AM WARM-HEARTED
French-Style Grilled Polenta with Mushroom Ragout

Polenta is a classic comfort food that we serve all year-round because it's uniquely satisfying and popular with our guests. Plus it's a rich but neutral base that gets along well with whatever dressings or sauces you want to layer over it. In the summer we stick with lighter options like bright puttanesca or pesto, in the winter we offer this hearty mushroom ragout layered with our Cashew Ricotta and peppery arugula. While I call for a two-step process of preparing the polenta and then grilling or searing it—which adds really pleasing texture and smoky, caramelized flavor—you could absolutely spoon the ragout over soft polenta and call it a meal.

SERVES 6 TO 8

For the Polenta:

1 tablespoon extra-virgin olive oil, plus more as needed

2 teaspoons Himalayan sea salt

2 cups medium-grind polenta

For the Mushroom Ragout:

3 tablespoons extra-virgin olive oil

¾ cup diced celery

¾ cup diced yellow onion

3 sprigs fresh thyme

1 sprig fresh rosemary

1 tablespoon chopped garlic

¼ cup red wine

6½ cups (about 1 pound) stemmed and sliced mushrooms (a mix of cremini and shiitake is great here)

1 tablespoon capers, drained

1 teaspoon Himalayan sea salt

1. Make the polenta: Oil a baking sheet with 1 teaspoon of the olive oil and set aside.

2. In a large pot over high heat, stir the salt and remaining 2 teaspoons olive oil into 6 cups of water and bring to a boil. Whisk in the polenta and immediately reduce the heat to a simmer. Continue whisking to break up any lumps of polenta. When smooth, switch to a long-handled wooden spoon and stir continuously for 5 to 7 minutes, until the polenta has softened but retains a pleasant bite.

3. Spoon the cooked polenta onto the prepared baking sheet, using the back of the wooden spoon to spread it in an even layer. You can spread a few drops of oil on the spoon or a spatula to keep the polenta from sticking to it too much.

4. Allow the polenta to cool and set for at least 1 hour and up to overnight in the fridge.

5. Make the mushroom ragout: In a large skillet over medium heat, heat the olive oil. Add the celery, onion, thyme, rosemary, and garlic and cook for 10 minutes, stirring

recipe and ingredients continue

For Serving:

Extra-virgin olive oil,
for brushing

4 cups arugula

1 cup Cashew Ricotta
(page 311)

½ cup Brazil Nut Parmesan
(page 317)

½ cup chopped fresh basil

frequently. Add the red wine and stir for 1 minute, scraping up any flavorful bits from the bottom of the pan.

6. Add the mushrooms, capers, and salt and stir to combine. Cook for 15 minutes, until the mushrooms have softened and given up much of their moisture. Remove the pan from the heat and cover to keep warm while you grill the polenta. Remove and discard the herb sprigs.

7. To serve: Preheat a grill, grill pan, or a large skillet over medium-high heat.

8. Brush the cooled polenta with a thin layer of olive oil and cut the polenta into 8 large squares. Grill or pan-fry the polenta squares for 3 to 4 minutes per side, until golden. Cut each grilled polenta square diagonally to make 16 total triangles.

9. You can serve this family style on a pretty platter or on individual dinner plates. Layer half of the arugula on the platter or plates, followed by half of the grilled polenta triangles, the remaining arugula, and the remaining polenta. Top with the mushroom ragout and drizzle with the cashew ricotta. Garnish with the Brazil nut Parmesan and basil.

I AM RESOLVED

Southern Sampler with Louisiana Red Beans and Rice, Blackened Tempeh, Cheddar-Jalapeño Biscuits, and Cajun Collards

Over the years, our kitchen has developed a surprising number of true-to-their-roots, Southern-inspired elements. We figured the best way to showcase them was by heaping them together on a plate, comfort food–style. Every piece here could just as easily stand on its own, though, so don't feel restricted by time or inclination. You could also do as we have done on our lunch menu and toss everything over rice and call it a bowl.

SERVES 4

For the Smashed Maple Yams:

4 pounds garnet yams, peeled and cut into 2-inch chunks

1 tablespoon extra-virgin olive oil

1 teaspoon Himalayan sea salt

¼ cup white or yellow miso

¼ cup fresh orange juice

2 tablespoons toasted sesame oil

2 tablespoons molasses

2 tablespoons maple syrup

1 tablespoon fresh lemon juice

1½ teaspoons tamari

⅛ teaspoon ground cinnamon

For the Cheddar-Jalapeño Biscuits:

½ cup Macadamia Cheddar (page 316)

2 cups all-purpose flour, plus more for dusting

1. Make the smashed maple yams: Preheat the oven to 400°F.

2. In a large bowl, combine the yams, olive oil, and salt. Toss to coat. Spread the yams out in a single layer on a baking sheet (use 2 if necessary) and roast for 20 to 30 minutes, until the yams are soft and beginning to caramelize. Remove the yams from the oven but leave the oven on.

3. In a blender, combine the miso, orange juice, sesame oil, molasses, maple syrup, lemon juice, tamari, and cinnamon and blend until smooth.

4. In a large bowl, combine the warm roasted yams with the marinade and toss to coat. Spread the yams back out onto the baking sheet(s) and roast for an additional 8 to 10 minutes, until the marinade is mostly absorbed.

5. In a large bowl, mash the yams to a rough, chunky texture.

6. Make the cheddar-jalapeño biscuits: On a small plate, spread out the macadamia cheddar into about a ¼-inch layer. Place in the freezer for at least 1 hour, until the cheese is completely frozen. Cut the frozen cheese into ¼-inch cubes and set aside.

recipe and ingredients continue

2 tablespoons baking powder

1 tablespoon cane sugar

1 teaspoon Himalayan sea salt

¼ cup plus 1 tablespoon vegan butter

¾ cup Almond Milk (page 30) or store-bought, plus more for finishing

½ to 1 small jalapeño, seeded and finely chopped

For the Cajun Collards:

1½ tablespoons extra-virgin olive oil

2 bunches collard greens, stemmed and roughly chopped

¼ cup white wine

½ teaspoon Himalayan sea salt

½ teaspoon Cajun seasoning (we like Frontier)

For Serving:

2 cups cooked brown rice

2 cups canned red beans, drained and rinsed

1 tablespoon Cajun seasoning

1 teaspoon Gremolata (page 293)

1 recipe Blackened Tempeh (see page 199), cut into ½-inch slices

2 scallions (white and green parts), chopped

1 cup Creamy Mexican Coleslaw (see page 175)

Barbecue Sauce (page 307), as desired

7. In the bowl of a food processor, combine the flour, baking powder, sugar, and salt. Pulse briefly to combine. Add the vegan butter and pulse until the mixture becomes shaggy and dry and begins to hold together in some places. (You can also do this part by hand with a fork or pastry cutter.)

8. Transfer the flour mixture to a large mixing bowl and add the almond milk, jalapeño, and macadamia cheddar pieces. Gently stir with a fork until the mixture forms a ball.

9. Turn the dough out onto a floured surface. Using lightly floured hands, gently pat the dough into a 10-inch x 6-inch rectangle, about 1 inch thick. Fold the dough in half, then in half again. Pat this back down into another roughly 10-inch x 6-inch rectangle. Cover the dough with a clean towel and let the dough sit at room temperature for 30 minutes.

10. Preheat the oven to 425°F. Line a baking sheet with parchment paper and set aside.

11. Using a 3-inch biscuit cutter or floured glass, cut the dough into 8 biscuits. Try to avoid twisting the cutter or glass, as this will inhibit the biscuits' ability to rise.

12. Place the biscuits on the lined baking sheet and brush each one with a small amount of almond milk. Bake for 10 to 15 minutes, until golden brown. Set aside.

13. Make the Cajun collards: Heat the olive oil in a large skillet over medium-high heat. Add as much of the collard greens as will fit in the pan, stirring to wilt slightly, and repeat until all of the greens are in the pan. Add the white wine, salt, and Cajun seasoning. Stir until the greens are completely wilted, 3 to 5 more minutes.

14. Serve: In a medium bowl, combine the rice, beans, Cajun seasoning, and gremolata and mix thoroughly. Place the beans and rice in the center of a large platter. Surround them with the sliced tempeh, smashed yams, collard greens, and biscuits. Garnish with the scallions and serve with Mexican coleslaw and barbecue sauce.

I AM BOUNTIFUL
Pasta with Smoky Tempeh Bolognese and Brazil Nut Parmesan

If there was one lesson I learned while cooking in Italy, it was how to tease the most flavor out of humble ingredients. Making a traditional Bolognese is the perfect example of the labor of love in the kitchen—it's a long, slow process that infuses an otherwise simple sauce with deep, rich flavor. But in this case, because we're using tempeh instead of meat, I had to figure out how to impart that same special quality. I discovered that by applying the shared principle of fully and thoroughly browning your ingredients—and I mean *brown*—you can achieve that flavorful, satisfying effect. I recommend sourcing a high-quality gluten-free or bean pasta for this (we use Andean Dream, a quinoa–brown rice mix), but a nice artisanal pasta would also do just fine. I tend to go for the shells because of the way they cradle the sauce, though a wide-cut fettuccine would also be really nice here.

SERVES 6

For the Tempeh Bolognese:

2 tablespoons extra-virgin olive oil

1 tablespoon Compassionate Blend (page 26)

1 celery stalk, finely chopped

1 small carrot, finely chopped

½ red onion, finely chopped

1 block Blackened Tempeh (see page 199), crumbled

¼ cup chopped cremini mushrooms

⅓ cup white wine

4 cups Marinara Sauce (page 212)

½ teaspoon smoked sea salt

1. Make the tempeh Bolognese: Heat the oil in a large pot or large, deep skillet over medium-high heat. Add the compassionate blend and cook for 1 minute, breaking it up with the back of a wooden spoon, until the oil begins taking on a reddish color.

2. Add the celery, carrot, and red onion and sauté until softened, 5 minutes. Add the crumbled tempeh and the mushrooms and cook for 5 minutes, until the mixture has browned and begins sticking to the bottom of the pot. Stir in the wine while scraping the bottom of the pot to loosen up the flavorful bits. Add the marinara, smoked salt, and ½ cup of water and bring the sauce to a simmer. Reduce the heat to low and continue simmering, partially covered, for 20 minutes, until the sauce comes together.

recipe and ingredients continue

To Assemble:

6 cups baby spinach

¼ cup extra-virgin olive oil

3 garlic cloves, chopped

1 bunch broccolini, chopped

1 teaspoon Himalayan sea salt

¼ cup white wine

1 pound pasta of choice, cooked according to package instructions

2 cups Cashew Mozzarella (page 312)

1 cup Brazil Nut Parmesan (page 317)

½ cup chopped fresh basil

3. Assemble the pasta: Place the baby spinach in a large serving bowl and set aside.

4. Heat the olive oil in a large, deep skillet over medium-high heat. Add the garlic and sauté just until the garlic is fragrant, less than 1 minute. Add the broccolini and salt and cook until the broccolini starts to become tender, about 5 minutes. Stir in the white wine and simmer until the alcohol has cooked off, about 2 minutes.

5. Add the pasta to the skillet and toss with the broccolini. Once the pasta is warmed through, about 2 minutes, pour the pasta-broccolini mixture into the serving bowl over the spinach. Give everything a good toss so all of the spinach wilts. Top with the Bolognese and lightly toss so the Bolognese begins to meld with the pasta. Crumble the cashew mozzarella over the top, followed by the Parmesan and a sprinkling of fresh basil. Serve hot.

Eggplant Caponata Pasta

SERVES 4

This is our summer version of I Am Bountiful, which features our eggplant caponata tossed with an heirloom tomato sauce and arugula. It's a lovely, light meal that can be served hot or cold.

For the Braised Cherry Tomato Sauce:

¼ cup extra-virgin olive oil

2 garlic cloves, chopped

2 pints of cherry tomatoes (about 1½ pounds), halved (heirloom cherry tomatoes are great if you can find them)

¾ teaspoon Himalayan sea salt

For the Pasta:

4 cups baby arugula

2 tablespoons extra-virgin olive oil

1 pound quinoa pasta (or your favorite pasta), cooked according to package instructions

1 recipe Eggplant Caponata (page 94)

¼ cup white wine

Red chili flakes (optional)

¼ cup Brazil Nut Parmesan (page 317)

¼ cup fresh basil leaves, torn or chopped

1. Make the braised cherry tomato sauce: Heat the olive oil in a large skillet over medium heat. Add the garlic and sauté until the garlic is fragrant and starting to turn golden, about 1 minute. Raise the heat to medium-high and add the tomatoes and salt. Cook, stirring and tossing frequently, until the tomatoes are softened but still hold their shape, about 5 minutes.

2. Assemble the pasta: Arrange the arugula on a large serving platter and set aside.

3. Heat the olive oil in a large skillet or pot over medium-high heat. Add the pasta and toss to coat it in the oil. Add the caponata and toss until warmed through, 2 to 3 minutes. Pour in the white wine and cook until the alcohol has cooked off, about 3 minutes. Stir in the braised cherry tomatoes and chili flakes, if using. Toss and cook until heated through, 2 to 3 minutes. Spoon the mixture over the arugula on the serving platter and garnish with the Parmesan and basil.

DESSERTS

THE GRATITUDE CLASSICS

I AM OPEN
Gluten-Free Lemon Blueberry Coffee Cake

Perfect for a light dessert or an afternoon snack, this is somewhere between a coffee cake and a pound cake. The lemon and blueberry combination is classic, each really accentuating each other's best qualities—the citrus brings out the brightness of the blueberries, while the berries deliver balance with their sweetness. The cake itself is moist and dense, so don't be afraid when you pull it out of the oven and it looks underdone. And definitely don't be tempted to overbake—dry and crumbly isn't what you're going for.

MAKES ONE 9-INCH CAKE

For the Crumb Topping:

1 cup unsweetened coconut flakes

¾ cup Gluten-Free All-Purpose Bakery Flour Blend (page 34)

¼ cup coconut sugar

¼ cup coconut oil, melted

¼ cup fresh lemon juice

⅛ teaspoon vanilla extract

For the Cake Batter:

½ cup coconut oil, melted and cooled, plus more for the pan

¼ cup ground flaxseed

2 cups Gluten-Free All-Purpose Bakery Flour Blend (page 34)

½ cup coconut sugar

½ teaspoon Himalayan sea salt

½ teaspoon lemon zest

¼ teaspoon ground cardamom

1½ cups Coconut Yogurt (page 33) or store-bought

⅓ cup fresh lemon juice

1. Make the crumb topping: In a medium bowl, combine the coconut flakes, flour blend, coconut sugar, coconut oil, lemon juice, and vanilla. Mix gently to form a crumbly mixture. Set aside.

2. Make the cake batter: Preheat the oven to 325°F. Prepare a 9-inch square cake pan with coconut oil or cooking spray and set aside.

3. In a medium bowl, whisk together the ground flaxseed with ½ cup of warm water. Set aside for 5 minutes to let the mixture jell while you prepare the other ingredients.

4. In a large bowl, combine the flour blend, coconut sugar, salt, lemon zest, and cardamom. Set aside.

5. Once the flaxseeds have jelled, whisk in the coconut yogurt, ½ cup coconut oil, lemon juice, and vanilla. Add the flax-yogurt mixture to the dry ingredients and mix until just combined. Add ½ cup of the blueberries and gently smash them into the mixture. This will give the cake a nice swirl of color. Gently fold in the remaining 1 cup whole blueberries.

6. Add half of the cake batter to the prepared pan in an even layer. Top the batter with half of the crumb topping. Repeat

recipe and ingredients continue

¼ teaspoon vanilla extract

1½ cups fresh blueberries, plus more for garnish

For the Lemon Glaze:

½ cup powdered sugar

1 tablespoon fresh lemon juice, plus more if needed

with the other half of the cake batter and crumb mixture. You can gently tap or slide the pan back and forth on a counter to ensure the mixture settles evenly in the pan. Bake for 50 minutes to 1 hour, until the cake is golden and a tester comes out clean. Tent the cake with foil if it begins to get too dark. Allow the cake to cool completely in the pan while you make the glaze.

7. Make the lemon glaze: In a small bowl, whisk together the powdered sugar and lemon juice. It will come together as a thick mixture, but you can add an additional 1 to 2 teaspoons of lemon juice for a runnier glaze.

8. Remove the cooled cake from the pan and set it on a plate or platter. Drizzle the lemon glaze on the top of the coffee cake and add some whole blueberries for decoration.

NOTE There are two rules that I follow in vegan baking: Do not overmix your batter and do not let your batter sit too long before getting it into the oven. Ignoring either or both of these rules will result in a final product that is denser than it needs to be.

I AM PASSIONATE
Black Lava Cake

It took a little bit of work on our part to replicate the signature oozy, warm chocolate-filled cake in a vegan format. But I can honestly tell you that we nailed it, complete with caramel sauce and caramelized almonds. It requires a little planning ahead, because the batter needs to set up in the refrigerator, but it's worth the wait. It's a cake that really has an effect on people.

SERVES 6

For the Black Lava Cake:

½ cup chopped bittersweet baking chocolate

¼ cup raw cacao powder, plus more for dusting

¼ cup coconut sugar

2 tablespoons coconut oil, plus more for ramekins

¼ teaspoon vanilla extract

¼ teaspoon Himalayan sea salt

1 cup Almond Milk (page 30) or store-bought

¼ cup Gluten-Free All-Purpose Bakery Flour Blend (page 34)

½ teaspoon baking powder

¾ cup vegan chocolate chips

For the Caramel Sauce:

¼ cup cashews, soaked overnight

2 tablespoons coconut butter or coconut manna

½ teaspoon Himalayan sea salt

¾ cup cane sugar

¼ cup coconut sugar

⅓ cup vegan butter

1. Make the black lava cake: In a medium saucepan over medium-high heat, bring 1 cup of water to a simmer. Add the baking chocolate to a medium heatproof bowl and place it over—but not touching—the simmering water. Gently stir the chocolate until most of it has melted. Remove the bowl from the heat and continue stirring until all of the chocolate is completely melted and smooth.

2. In a food processor, combine the melted chocolate, cacao powder, coconut sugar, coconut oil, vanilla, and salt and process until smooth. Add the almond milk and continue processing until incorporated. Add the flour blend and baking powder and process until the mixture is smooth and uniform.

3. Prepare six 4-ounce ramekins by greasing them lightly with coconut oil and dusting with cacao powder. Add ⅓ cup of the lava cake mixture into each prepared ramekin and refrigerate for 1 hour.

4. After the ramekins have chilled, create an opening in the center of each cake by gently pushing the cake batter to the sides. Place 2 tablespoons of the chocolate chips in each opening. Replace the batter to seal over the chocolate chips. Return the ramekins to the refrigerator for at least 2 more hours.

5. Make the caramel sauce: In a blender, combine the cashews, coconut butter or manna, salt, and ½ cup plus

recipe and ingredients continue

For the Caramelized Almonds:

½ cup cane sugar

1 cup whole raw almonds

2 tablespoons vegan butter

2 tablespoons of water and blend until a smooth, thick cream forms. Set aside.

6. In a medium saucepan over medium heat, combine the cane sugar, coconut sugar, and 1 tablespoon of water. Heat the mixture, stirring occasionally, until it becomes a syrup, about 10 minutes. Allow the syrup to continue to boil, now refraining from stirring, until it becomes a dark brown caramel, 3 to 5 more minutes. Immediately remove the pan from the heat.

7. Whisk the cashew cream into the caramel and return the pan to the heat. Cook the mixture over medium heat, stirring occasionally, until the mixture is at a rolling boil and has reduced to where a thick ribbon will drizzle from a spoon, 5 to 8 minutes. Remove the pan from the heat and stir in the butter. Set aside to cool.

8. Make the caramelized almonds: Line a baking sheet with parchment paper and set aside.

9. In a medium, heavy-bottomed pot over medium heat, combine the cane sugar with 2 tablespoons of water and bring to a boil. Add the almonds and mix with a silicone spatula or wooden spoon until the syrup crystallizes around the almonds, about 5 minutes. Add the vegan butter and continue stirring over medium heat until the almond coating becomes a golden-brown caramel, 3 more minutes. Once the crystallized sugar has completely melted, remove the pot from the heat and spread the nut mixture over the prepared baking sheet. Set aside to cool completely before breaking up any large clusters of nuts with your hands.

10. Preheat the oven to 325°F.

11. Bake the cakes until they are set around the edges, 15 to 20 minutes, then allow them to cool for at least 2 minutes. Run a small spatula or knife around the sides of each ramekin and flip each cake onto a small plate. Drizzle with the caramel, top with the caramelized almonds, and dust the plate with cacao powder. Alternatively, serve the cakes in the ramekins.

I AM LOVELY
Gluten-Free Peach and Berry Cobbler

This is a guilt-free spin on the essential summertime dessert, best prepared (in my opinion) in unapologetically rustic fashion with the gluten-free biscuit filling poured over the top, baked until golden, and served with plenty of spoons.

For best results, I've found that letting your fruit marinate for 4 hours is helpful, as the lemon juice and sugar soften the fruit slightly while accentuating the fullest expression of its flavor. That said, this step isn't wholly necessary, making this dessert perfect for whipping up at a moment's notice.

SERVES 6

For the Fruit Filling:

7½ cups sliced peaches and mixed berries

3 tablespoons coconut sugar

1½ tablespoons Gluten-Free All-Purpose Bakery Flour Blend (page 34)

1 tablespoon fresh orange juice

1 tablespoon fresh lemon juice

Zest of 1 lemon or orange

¼ teaspoon Himalayan sea salt

¼ teaspoon vanilla extract

For the Gluten-Free Biscuit Batter:

½ cup Gluten-Free All-Purpose Bakery Flour Blend (page 34)

2 tablespoons coconut sugar, plus more for sprinkling

¼ teaspoon Himalayan sea salt

⅔ cup Coconut Milk (page 32) or store-bought

2 tablespoons coconut oil, melted, plus more for pan

1. Make the fruit filling: In a large bowl, combine the fruit, coconut sugar, flour blend, orange juice, lemon juice, lemon or orange zest, salt, and vanilla. Mix gently but thoroughly to ensure that the fruit is evenly coated.

2. Cover the bowl and allow the fruit to macerate in the refrigerator for at least 1 hour and up to 4 hours.

3. Make the gluten-free biscuit batter: In a medium bowl, whisk together the flour blend, coconut sugar, and salt. Add the coconut milk and 2 tablespoons coconut oil and whisk until smooth.

4. Preheat the oven to 325°F. Oil an 11-inch x 7-inch baking pan with coconut oil or other light cooking oil of choice.

5. Pour the fruit and juices into the prepared pan and spoon or drizzle the biscuit batter over the top. Sprinkle the surface with coconut sugar to give it a nice golden color as it bakes. Bake for 25 minutes, or until the fruit is bubbling and the topping is golden brown.

I AM KIND
Crispy Quinoa Bars

People often ask me if I spend all day grazing from the Gratitude menu. While, like most chefs, I'm busier cooking than I am snacking, these bars would be the one exception. If there's a batch in the bakery case, I'm liable to grab one on my way out the door. They're technically a healthier take on the traditional Rice Krispies Treats, but I find them far more pleasing due to their more subtle sweetness, crunch from the puffed quinoa, and decadent chocolate drizzle.

MAKES 12 BARS

5 cups puffed quinoa or puffed brown rice cereal

1½ teaspoons coconut sugar

½ teaspoon Himalayan sea salt

½ cup cacao butter

⅓ cup coconut butter or coconut manna

⅔ cup almond butter

½ cup coconut nectar

1 teaspoon vanilla extract

1 cup chopped (10 ounces) bittersweet chocolate

1. In a large bowl, combine the puffed quinoa or rice, coconut sugar, and salt. Set aside.

2. Line a 9- x 13-inch baking pan with parchment paper, leaving a few inches of excess on either side. (This will come in handy for lifting the bars out later.) Set aside.

3. In a small saucepan over low heat, combine the cacao butter and coconut butter or manna. Gently stir the butters while they melt completely, about 2 minutes. Remove the pan from the heat and add the almond butter, coconut nectar, and vanilla. Stir until the almond butter has softened in the residual heat and the mixture is well combined.

4. Pour the warm coconut–almond butter mixture over the dry ingredients and mix gently with a wooden spoon or spatula until just combined. Press the mixture into the prepared pan and use a spatula to smooth the surface. Refrigerate for 2 hours, or until set.

5. Line a baking sheet with parchment paper.

6. Lift the bars out of the pan using the sides of the parchment paper as handles. Transfer them to a cutting board and cut them into 12 bars. Arrange the bars on the parchment-lined baking sheet, leaving 2 inches between each bar.

recipe continues

7. In a medium saucepan over medium-high heat, bring 1 cup of water to a boil. Place the chocolate in a medium heatproof bowl and set the bowl over—but not touching—the simmering water. Stir the chocolate with a spatula, turning it occasionally so it melts evenly. When most of the chocolate is melted, remove the bowl from the pan and continue stirring the chocolate off the heat until it has fully melted.

8. Using a spoon or spatula, drizzle the melted chocolate over the bars in whatever design you like. Return the tray of bars to the refrigerator for 2 more hours before serving. Store these bars in an airtight container in the refrigerator to prevent them from becoming too soft.

QUESTION *of the day* / What is one thing you would love to fulfill in your lifetime?

I AM DIVINE
Strawberry Shortcake in a Jar

It doesn't get more divine than individual jars filled with light gluten-free cake layered between coconut-cashew whipped cream and strawberry chia jam. These are perfectly transportable, making them great for picnics and potlucks.

The super-easy strawberry jam comes together in about 45 minutes, thanks to those chia seeds! Normally you have to reduce jam for quite a bit longer, but for this version you only need the strawberries to soften and give up their juices, which the chias soak up to essentially set the jam. It may be a bit looser than you're used to, but it drapes perfectly over the layers of this confection.

SERVES 4

For the Shortcake:
3 tablespoons coconut oil, melted and slightly cooled, plus more for the pan
½ cup Almond Milk (page 30) or store-bought
½ teaspoon apple cider vinegar
¾ cup Gluten-Free All-Purpose Bakery Flour Blend (page 34)
¼ cup cane sugar
½ teaspoon baking powder
¼ teaspoon baking soda
¼ teaspoon vanilla extract

For the Strawberry Chia Jam:
2 cups fresh strawberries, hulled
2 tablespoons cane sugar
1 tablespoon fresh lemon juice
1 tablespoon chia seeds

1. Make the shortcake: Preheat the oven to 325°F. Prepare 4 cups of a muffin pan with coconut oil or cooking spray.

2. In a small bowl, combine the almond milk and apple cider vinegar and set aside for a few minutes.

3. In a large bowl, add the flour blend, sugar, baking powder, and baking soda. Using a spatula, mix together the dry ingredients, then stir in the almond milk–vinegar mixture. Add the vanilla and the 3 tablespoons coconut oil and continue mixing until just combined.

4. Fill the greased cups in the muffin pan each about ¾ full of batter, making sure the batter is evenly distributed among the cups. Bake for about 14 minutes, or until golden. Let the shortcakes cool completely in the pan.

5. Make the strawberry chia jam: Slice the strawberries in halves or quarters, depending on their size.

6. In a medium pot over medium heat, combine the strawberries, sugar, and lemon juice. Cook for 15 minutes, stirring frequently. The strawberries should be softened but not completely disintegrated. Remove the pot from the heat

recipe and ingredients continue

To Assemble:

½ cup Almond Milk (page 30) or store-bought

2 tablespoons maple syrup

Pinch of Himalayan sea salt

Four 8-ounce Mason jars

1 cup Cashew Whipped Cream (see page 263)

Chopped fresh strawberries (optional)

and transfer the mixture to a medium bowl. Stir in the chia seeds and let the jam cool in the refrigerator to set, about 30 minutes.

7. Assemble the jars: In a medium bowl, stir together the almond milk, maple syrup, and salt.

8. Cut the cooled shortcakes horizontally into equal halves. Briefly soak the bottom half of a shortcake in the almond milk mixture and place it at the bottom of one of the Mason jars. Spoon 2 tablespoons of the strawberry chia jam onto the shortcake and top with 2 tablespoons of the whipped cream. Soak the top half of the shortcake in the almond milk and crumble it gently with your fingers into the jar. Add another layer of the jam and whipped cream as before. The jam and whipped cream are soft enough where they should spread out by themselves, but you can tap the jar gently to encourage them to spread out and create an even layer.

9. Garnish with chopped strawberries, if desired. Repeat with the remaining shortcakes. These can be stored in the refrigerator overnight, if desired.

I AM SENSATIONAL
Persimmon Pudding

This sits somewhere between a traditional pudding and a bread pudding and is, frankly, a contribution to mankind. We call for using a Hachiya persimmon, as they come into season in the fall, which lends its deep sweetness. Served warm with your favorite vegan ice cream, this is one gorgeous offering.

SERVES 4

¼ cup plus 1 teaspoon coconut oil, melted and cooled

2 tablespoons ground flaxseed

¾ cup Gluten-Free All-Purpose Bakery Flour Blend (page 34)

¾ cup coconut sugar, plus more for sprinkling

½ teaspoon baking powder

¼ teaspoon Himalayan sea salt

¼ teaspoon baking soda

¼ teaspoon ground cinnamon

1 very ripe Hachiya persimmon

¾ cup Almond Milk (page 30) or store-bought

1½ teaspoons apple cider vinegar

1. Preheat the oven to 350°F. Oil four 8-ounce ramekins or oven-safe mugs with ¼ teaspoon each of the coconut oil.

2. In a small bowl, whisk together the ground flaxseed and ¼ cup warm water. Allow the mixture to sit for about 5 minutes. It will become gelatinous and viscous, serving as a binder in this recipe.

3. In a medium bowl, sift together the flour blend, coconut sugar, baking powder, salt, baking soda, and cinnamon. Use a spoon or your hands to scoop the flesh from the persimmon into the bowl. Discard the stem and skin. Add the almond milk, apple cider vinegar, and flax mixture and fold gently to combine. Add the remaining ¼ cup melted coconut oil and gently fold in once more.

4. Fill each ramekin about ⅔ full with the mixture and sprinkle some coconut sugar over the top. Bake for 25 to 30 minutes, until the puddings are springy to the touch and a toothpick inserted into the centers comes out clean.

5. Serve warm or at room temperature, ideally with your favorite vegan ice cream.

I AM SUPER
Bittersweet Chocolate Nuggets

These bites have the beautiful, dark intensity of a chocolate truffle but all the benefits of superfoods raw cacao and maca. They're an energy pick-me-up while fulfilling the urge for something sweet.

MAKES 12 NUGGETS

1 cup raw cacao nibs

¼ cup raw cacao powder

1½ teaspoons maca powder

½ teaspoon Himalayan sea salt

⅓ cup almond butter

3 tablespoons coconut nectar

2 tablespoons coconut butter or coconut manna, melted

¼ teaspoon vanilla extract

1. In a clean coffee or spice grinder, grind the cacao nibs until very fine. (Depending on the size of your grinder, you may want to do this in batches.)

2. In a medium bowl, combine the ground cacao nibs, cacao powder, maca, and salt. Add the almond butter, coconut nectar, coconut butter, and vanilla and use your hands to mix until thoroughly combined. The mixture will be quite sticky, so using your hands versus a spoon is helpful in making sure that everything is consistently blended.

3. Using a small ice-cream scoop or melon baller, form the mixture into 12 balls and arrange them on a plate or tray. The nuggets can be served immediately or refrigerated briefly to firm up. Store in an airtight container at room temperature for up to 3 days.

NOTE You can replace the maca powder with any powdered superfood (camu camu, ashwagandha, reishi). For a yummy spicy version, add ½ teaspoon of cayenne, or to taste.

I AM AFFECTIONATE
Chocolate Chip Walnut Cookies

We've done a few different versions of the ultimate vegan cookie over the years, but the all-time winner is the chocolate chip–walnut. It's a big, chewy, whole-food treat that just really hits the spot.

MAKES 12 COOKIES

¾ cup Gluten-Free All-Purpose Bakery Flour Blend (page 34)

¾ cup vegan semisweet chocolate chips

½ cup raw walnuts, chopped

½ cup rolled oats

½ cup cane sugar

1 teaspoon baking powder

¾ teaspoon ground cinnamon

½ teaspoon Himalayan sea salt

¼ teaspoon baking soda

⅓ cup Coconut Milk (page 32) or store-bought

⅓ cup maple syrup

1 tablespoon chia seeds

¼ cup coconut oil, softened

½ cup almond butter

1. Preheat the oven to 325°F. Line two baking sheets with parchment paper and set aside.

2. In a large bowl, combine the flour blend, chocolate chips, walnuts, oats, sugar, baking powder, cinnamon, salt, and baking soda. Mix gently until combined.

3. In a blender, combine the coconut milk, maple syrup, and chia seeds. Blend until the chia is fully dissolved, about 1 minute. Add the wet blended mix to the dry mix, along with the coconut oil and almond butter. Mix until everything is fully incorporated and forms a soft dough.

4. Using a ¼-cup measure, scoop the dough onto the prepared baking sheets, spacing each cookie 5 inches apart, and flattening each cookie slightly. Bake for 20 to 25 minutes, until the edges are golden brown. Transfer to a cooling rack. The cookies should still be a little soft when you remove them, but they'll firm up as they cool. Store the cooled cookies in an airtight container at room temperature for up to 3 days.

I AM SACRED
Spiced Shortbread Cookies

These are a nod to the Mexican wedding cookie as well as a traditional shortbread cookie. They're indulgently dense while being very simple to make. And you can add whatever you like to flavor them all manner of ways—orange zest, currants, chocolate chips.

MAKES 16 COOKIES

1 cup Gluten-Free All-Purpose Bakery Flour Blend (page 34)

½ teaspoon ground nutmeg

½ teaspoon ground cinnamon

¼ teaspoon Himalayan sea salt

¼ teaspoon ground cloves

Zest of 1 lemon

¼ cup coconut oil

¼ cup powdered sugar, plus more for rolling

1 teaspoon grated fresh ginger

¼ teaspoon vanilla extract

½ cup raw pecans, chopped

1. Line a baking sheet with parchment paper and set aside.

2. In a medium bowl, add the flour blend, nutmeg, cinnamon, salt, cloves, and lemon zest. Mix gently with a spatula and set aside.

3. In the bowl of a stand mixer fitted with the paddle attachment, combine the coconut oil, powdered sugar, grated ginger, and vanilla plus 3 teaspoons of water and beat on low speed until well combined.

4. Add the dry ingredients about a third at a time, allowing them to incorporate thoroughly before adding more. Scrape down the bowl between additions to ensure everything is well combined. Once all of the dry ingredients have been added, mix in the pecans on low speed.

5. Scoop the dough onto the prepared baking sheet in roughly 2-tablespoon portions, spaced evenly, then gently flatten out each cookie to about ½ inch thick. Refrigerate the cookies for 10 minutes.

6. Preheat the oven to 350°F.

7. Bake the cookies for 20 minutes, until they are a light golden color. Rotate the baking sheet halfway through baking to ensure that the cookies bake evenly. Allow the cookies to cool on the pan completely before rolling them in powdered sugar. Store in an airtight container at room temperature for up to 1 week.

THE GRATITUDE CLASSICS

Our origins as a raw-food, vegan café are still laced through our menus, offering our customers the same beloved dishes that made Café Gratitude what it was fifteen years ago. The following desserts are from the original raw collection and continue to be ordered and adored. While these recipes don't call for traditional baking practices, the techniques aren't difficult and the results are vibrant, satisfying, and delicious.

I AM AWAKENING
Key Lime Pie

What's interesting about this pie—and is surprising to most people—is that the primary base of the key lime cream is avocado. It's the perfect silky, fatty texture that this otherwise light and bright dessert requires. This dessert is easy to put together, but it does require several hours in the refrigerator to set up. If you like, you can make extra whipped cream and refrigerate it overnight to make it thick and spreadable while the pie chills. (See photo, pp. 260–261.)

MAKES ONE 9-INCH PIE

For the Pecan Crust:

1 teaspoon coconut oil

1 cup raw pecans

2 tablespoons Date Paste (page 35)

Pinch of Himalayan sea salt

⅛ teaspoon vanilla extract

For the Key Lime Filling:

1½ cups smashed avocados

1 cup fresh lime juice (about 8 limes)

¾ cup agave nectar

⅔ cup Coconut Milk (page 32) or store-bought

¼ teaspoon Himalayan sea salt

⅛ teaspoon vanilla extract

1 cup coconut oil, melted

¼ cup soy or sunflower lecithin

1. Make the pecan crust: Lightly grease the entire inside of a 9-inch pie dish or pan with the coconut oil.

2. In a food processor, combine the pecans, date paste, and salt and process until the mixture begins to rise up the sides of the processor bowl. With the processor still running, stream in the vanilla plus 1 tablespoon of water, stopping occasionally to scrape down the sides. Process until the mixture holds together with gentle pressure and breaks apart cleanly.

3. Using your hands, press the pecan mixture into the bottom and sides of the dish or pan, creating an even crust. Set aside.

4. Make the key lime filling: In a blender, combine the avocados, lime juice, agave nectar, coconut milk, salt, and vanilla and blend until smooth and creamy. Add the coconut oil and lecithin and continue blending until the mixture is completely smooth. You may have to stop and scrape down the sides of the blender as you go.

5. Pour the lime filling into the prepared crust. Refrigerate the pie for about 1 hour, or until the filling is firm and set.

For the Cashew Whipped Cream:

1 cup raw cashews, soaked for 4 hours and drained

¼ cup cane sugar

¼ teaspoon Himalayan sea salt

½ cup coconut oil, melted

For Serving:

Thin lime wedges or twists

Whole raw pecans

6. Make the cashew whipped cream: In a blender, combine the cashews, sugar, salt, and 1½ cups of water and blend until smooth and creamy. Add the coconut oil and continue blending until the mixture is completely combined. This will yield about 2 cups of whipped cream. Pour all of the cream over the top of the chilled pie. Return the pie to the refrigerator for at least 8 hours or overnight.

7. Serve: Remove the pie from the dish or pan by running a small spatula around the sides of the pie and place on a serving plate. Decorate with the lime wedges and pecans. At that point you can pipe it on top of the pie with the other decorations.

QUESTION *of the day* / What makes you joyful?

I AM ADORING
Tiramisu

For not including the typical eggs, milk, and mascarpone cheese, this vegan and processed sugar-free version of the trademark Italian dessert still manages to be a more than worthy homage, delivering both creamy decadence and ethereal lightness. Instead of calling for a cookie or cake base, we repurpose our almond pulp left over from house-made almond milk and use it to make a biscuit, though you could use store-bought almond flour instead. You could also substitute a vegan ladyfinger or sponge cake recipe, if you prefer. You'll want to start this recipe the day before you'd like to serve it, as it takes at least 12 hours to set up.

MAKES ONE 9-INCH CAKE

For the Vanilla Espresso Cake:

⅓ cup plus 1 teaspoon coconut oil, melted

1½ cups Date Paste (page 35) (you may need 2 batches)

½ teaspoon Himalayan sea salt

¼ teaspoon vanilla extract

4½ cups store-bought almond flour or Almond Pulp (page 30)

¼ cup Almond Milk (page 30) or store-bought

¼ cup cold-pressed coffee or espresso

For the Chocolate Mousse:

½ ounce soaked Irish moss (see page 313), roughly chopped

1⅓ cups Almond Milk (page 30) or store-bought

¼ cup agave nectar

1. Make the vanilla espresso cake: Lightly grease a 9-inch springform pan with 1 teaspoon of the coconut oil and set aside.

2. In the bowl of a stand mixer fitted with the paddle attachment, combine the date paste, remaining ⅓ cup coconut oil, salt, and vanilla. Begin mixing at low speed and slowly increase to medium-high until the mixture is creamy and very smooth. This will take a few minutes.

3. Turn off the mixer and add the almond flour, almond milk, and coffee or espresso. Mix at low speed for about 5 minutes, stopping and scraping down the sides of the bowl as needed until all of the ingredients are well incorporated. The cake batter should be soft and light to the touch. Spread half of the cake batter in the prepared pan in an even, flat layer. Place the pan and the bowl with the remaining cake batter in the refrigerator while you prepare the chocolate mousse.

4. Make the chocolate mousse: In a blender, combine the Irish moss and ½ cup of the almond milk and blend on medium speed until the moss begins to create a thick jelly. Small bits of Irish moss may accumulate on the sides of the

recipe and ingredients continue

¼ cup Date Paste (page 35)

¼ cup raw cacao powder

¼ teaspoon vanilla extract

Pinch of Himalayan sea salt

⅓ cup coconut oil, melted

2 tablespoons soy or sunflower lecithin

1 recipe Cashew Whipped Cream (see page 263), chilled for at least 12 hours

For Serving:

¼ cup plus 2 tablespoons raw cacao powder

Whole or crushed almonds, for garnish (optional)

Whole coffee beans, for garnish (optional)

blender or under the lid. Stop occasionally to scrape them down using a spatula and continue blending until you have a smooth gelatin. Do not move on to the next step until the mixture is completely smooth, otherwise you will have small bits of Irish moss in your mousse.

5. Once the mixture is completely smooth, add the remaining ½ cup plus ⅓ cup almond milk, agave nectar, date paste, cacao powder, vanilla, and salt and blend until smooth and creamy. Add the coconut oil and lecithin and resume blending until fully incorporated.

6. Spread the mousse over the first cake layer in the pan. Place the entire pan in the freezer to allow the mousse to set, about 1 hour.

7. When the mousse feels firm, gently add the remainder of the cake batter for the second cake layer. Top with the cashew whipped cream, using a spatula to spread it evenly over the cake. Refrigerate, covered, for 12 hours to set up.

8. To serve: Remove the outer ring from the springform pan. Using a small sifter, gently sprinkle the cacao powder in an even layer over the top of the cake. It should completely cover the whipped cream frosting. Garnish with almonds and coffee beans, if desired.

I AM REMARKABLE
Chocolate Cherry Black Forest Cake

This 100 percent raw dessert still manages to be a rich, decadent incarnation of traditional black forest cake. We offer it in the spring when fresh cherries are available and at their peak sweetness and flavor.

MAKES ONE 9-INCH CAKE

For the Cherry Frosting:

1¼ cups cherries, pitted

¾ cup raw cashews, soaked for 8 hours or more, drained, and rinsed

¼ cup agave nectar

2 tablespoons fresh lemon juice

1 tablespoon beet juice

¼ teaspoon Himalayan sea salt

⅛ teaspoon vanilla extract

½ cup coconut oil, melted

1½ tablespoons soy or sunflower lecithin

For the Chocolate Cherry Cake:

⅓ cup coconut oil, melted, plus more for the pan

1 cup Date Paste (page 35)

¼ teaspoon Himalayan sea salt

⅛ teaspoon vanilla extract

4½ cups store-bought almond flour or Almond Pulp (page 30)

¾ cup raw cacao powder

¼ cup Almond Milk (page 30) or store-bought

2 tablespoons agave nectar

3 cups pitted and chopped cherries

1. Make the cherry frosting: In a blender, combine the cherries, cashews, agave, lemon juice, beet juice, salt, and vanilla plus 1 tablespoon of water and blend until smooth and creamy. Add the coconut oil and lecithin and blend again until the mixture is completely smooth. Set aside while you make the cake batter.

2. Make the chocolate cherry cake: Lightly grease a 9-inch springform pan with coconut oil and set aside.

3. In the bowl of a stand mixer fitted with the paddle attachment, combine the ⅓ cup coconut oil, date paste, salt, and vanilla plus 3 tablespoons of water. Begin mixing at a low speed and slowly increase to medium speed until the mixture is very smooth and creamy. This will take a few minutes.

4. Turn off the mixer and add the almond flour, cacao powder, almond milk, and agave nectar. Beat at low speed for about 5 minutes, stopping and cleaning the sides of the bowl as needed until all the ingredients are well incorporated. Slowly add 1 cup of the cherries and continue to mix on the lowest setting. You can also fold in the cherries with a spatula.

5. Add half of the cake batter to the prepared pan, using a spatula or spoon to create a smooth, even layer. Scatter 1 cup of the chopped cherries over the top of the batter, followed by half of the cherry frosting. If your frosting needs help

recipe and ingredients continue

1 recipe Cashew Whipped
Cream (see page 263),
chilled for 12 to 24 hours

Small bar of vegan dark
chocolate, for garnish

1 whole cherry, stem and
pit intact, for garnish

spreading out among the cherries, gently shimmy the pan
on the counter. Place the cake in the freezer to set for about
2 hours, or until the frosting feels firm.

6. Gently pour the remainder of the cake batter over the set
frosting. Scatter the remaining cup of chopped cherries over
the top, and finish with the remaining frosting. Place the cake
in the refrigerator (not freezer) to set for 2 more hours.

7. Serve: Remove the outer ring from the springform pan.
Using a small spatula (an offset spatula works great here),
spread three-quarters of the whipped cream all over the
top and sides of the cake. You can try to get the finish as
smooth as possible or go for a more rustic look and leave
textured waves.

8. Use a vegetable peeler to create shavings from the
chocolate bar and lightly press them onto the sides of the
cake. Decorate the top of the cake with the remaining
whipped cream (if desired), more chocolate shavings, and the
whole cherry.

QUESTION
of the day / Who could you thank today?

I AM IRRESISTIBLE
Chocolate Coconut Cream Pie

What's particularly notable about this pie—aside from its luscious texture and rich coconut and chocolate flavor—is that it's free of both tree nuts and refined sugar. Instead we look to dates, for their caramel-y sweetness, and use coconut in both the filling and the crust.

MAKES ONE 9-INCH PIE

For the Coconut Chocolate Crust:

Coconut oil, for pan

1 cup unsweetened coconut flakes

⅓ cup raw cacao powder

2 tablespoons Date Paste (page 35)

Pinch of Himalayan sea salt

⅛ teaspoon vanilla extract

For the Coconut Chocolate Filling:

3 cups Coconut Milk (page 32) or store-bought

1 cup chopped young Thai coconut meat, frozen and thawed, or fresh

1 cup Date Paste (page 35)

½ teaspoon vanilla extract

¼ teaspoon Himalayan sea salt

1¼ cups coconut oil, melted

¼ cup soy or sunflower lecithin

¼ cup raw cacao powder

For Serving:

2 cups unsweetened coconut flakes

1. Make the coconut chocolate crust: Lightly grease the entire inside of a 9-inch round cake pan with coconut oil and set aside.

2. In a food processor, combine the coconut flakes, cacao powder, date paste, and salt and process until the mixture starts to rise up the sides of the processor bowl. With the processor still running, slowly add the vanilla plus 2 tablespoons of water. You will need to periodically scrape down the sides to ensure everything is thoroughly combined. Process until the mixture holds together with gentle pressure and breaks apart cleanly.

3. Using your hands, gently press the crust mixture into the bottom of the prepared cake pan, creating an even surface. Set aside.

4. Make the coconut chocolate filling: In a blender, combine the coconut milk, coconut meat, date paste, vanilla, and salt. Add ¼ cup plus 3 tablespoons of water and blend into a smooth cream. Add the coconut oil and lecithin and continue blending until the mixture is smooth and creamy, stopping the blender, if needed, to scrape down the sides.

5. Pour 4 cups of the filling on top of the prepared crust and keep the remaining 2 cups in the blender.

6. Add the cacao powder and 3 tablespoons of water to the remaining filling mixture. Blend the mixture until the cacao is just incorporated. Be careful not to overblend or it will be harder to swirl in.

7. Slowly pour 1½ cups of the chocolate filling into the coconut filling in the pan, moving the pan around to evenly distribute it. Pour the remainder of the chocolate filling very gently on the surface of the other fillings—it should sit right on top. Now you're ready to swirl!

8. Insert a chopstick or knife just below the surface of the filling and begin moving it around, swirling the 2 mixtures into each other. Try to swirl it so both colors are equally visible and create a marbled effect when the pie is sliced. For this it's better to swirl too little than too much! If the fillings are overblended they'll lose the contrast in color. Place the pie in the refrigerator for at least 6 hours to set.

9. Serve: Gently remove the pie from the pan using a small, thin spatula and place on a serving plate. Lightly press the coconut flakes around the sides and top edges.

DRESSINGS,
SAUCES
& DIPS

Harissa

Roasted Tomatillo Sauce

Goji Chipotle
Dressing

Matcha

Guacamole

Hollandaise

Avocado Cream

Mole Coloradito

Lucky Vinaigrette

Adobo de
Mixiote

Black Mole
Abuelita

Cashew Caesar
Dressing

Harissa

Mint Chutney

Toasted Almond
Romesco

Cilantro Pumpkin Seed Pesto

Sun-dried Tomato Pesto

Cashew Nacho Cheese

Basil Hempseed Pesto

Raw Zucchini Cilantro Hummus

Sesame Wasabi Sauce

Spicy Tomato Jam

Chipotle Ketchup

Garlic Tahini Dressing

Creamy Hempseed Ranch Dressing

Salsa Verde

Almond Thai Dressing

CASHEW CAESAR DRESSING

There are two types of Caesar dressings: those that are oil-based and anchovy-forward (or a vegan version thereof), and those that are on the creamier side. This is the latter. It's completely oil-free, but it still manages to be luscious and creamy with great garlicky flavor.

MAKES 2½ CUPS

1 cup raw cashews, soaked for 4 hours or overnight

2 tablespoons pumpkin seeds, soaked for 4 hours or overnight

⅓ cup fresh lemon juice

2 garlic cloves

1 teaspoon Himalayan salt

½ teaspoon freshly ground black pepper

Drain and rinse the cashews. In a blender, combine the cashews, pumpkin seeds, lemon juice, garlic, salt, and pepper with 1 cup of water. Blend on medium speed until the mixture is smooth and creamy. Store in the refrigerator for up to 1 week.

GOJI CHIPOTLE DRESSING

This is one of our original raw food recipes, and yet one of our most delicious thick and creamy dressings. It has a citrus tanginess that plays off of the smoky spiciness of the chipotle powder, not unlike a really great Thousand Island dressing.

MAKES 1 CUP

2 tablespoons pumpkin seeds, soaked for 4 hours or overnight

1 tablespoon dried goji berries, soaked for 4 hours or overnight

⅓ cup fresh orange juice

2 tablespoons fresh lime juice

1 Medjool date, pitted

¾ teaspoon Himalayan sea salt

¼ teaspoon chipotle powder

¼ cup extra-virgin olive oil

1. Drain and rinse the pumpkin seeds and goji berries.

2. In a blender, combine the soaked pumpkin seeds and goji berries with the orange juice, lime juice, date, salt, and chipotle powder and blend until smooth. With the blender running on medium speed, slowly drizzle in the olive oil and blend until fully emulsified. Store in the refrigerator for up to 1 week.

QUESTION *of the day* / How could you be of service today?

GARLIC TAHINI DRESSING

One of our original dressings from the early days of Café Gratitude. We use raw tahini, so the flavor profile is slightly lighter and brighter than what you'd expect from a tahini dressing, and we make mountains of it every day because it's one of those extremely versatile condiments that you can use in many ways other than on straight-up Mediterranean dishes. You'll see the parsley is stirred in at the end to maintain nice flecks of fresh herbs versus a solid green result.

MAKES 1½ CUPS

½ cup extra-virgin olive oil

Juice of 1 lemon

2 tablespoons sunflower seeds, soaked for 2 hours, drained, and rinsed

2 garlic cloves

1½ tablespoons sesame tahini, raw is great if you can find it

¼ teaspoon Himalayan sea salt

¼ cup chopped fresh parsley

In a blender, combine the olive oil, lemon juice, sunflower seeds, garlic, tahini, salt, and 3 tablespoons of water and blend until smooth. Pour the dressing into a medium bowl and stir in the parsley. Store in the refrigerator for up to 3 days.

Goji Chipotle Dressing
(page 278)

Sesame Wasabi Sauce
(page 299)

Gomasio
(page 27)

Almond Thai
Dressing
(opposite)

Avocado Cream
(page 97)

ALMOND THAI DRESSING

This is one of those rich, creamy, slightly spicy dressings that can be whatever you want it to be. It's just as delicious tossed with kelp noodles for Pad Thai or poured over a rice bowl as a peanut-sauce alternative. I particularly love it paired with roasted or sautéed vegetables, especially steamed greens.

MAKES 2 CUPS

½ cup almond butter

½ cup fresh cilantro leaves

½ cup fresh basil leaves

¼ cup fresh lemon juice

¼ jalapeño, seeded

2 tablespoons fresh ginger juice or 2 teaspoons dried ground ginger mixed with 2 tablespoons of water

1 tablespoon tamari

2 teaspoons agave nectar

1 teaspoon Himalayan sea salt

In a blender, combine the almond butter, cilantro, basil, lemon juice, jalapeño, ginger juice, tamari, agave nectar, salt, and ¾ cup of water. Blend until smooth. Store in the refrigerator for up to 3 days.

FIG BALSAMIC DRESSING

Even though we use whole dried figs as a thickener, this dressing isn't as sweet as you'd think. It's an Italian-style flavor profile that's extremely versatile and can be used to add flavor to vegetables (such as the eggplant in our Baked Eggplant Parmesan Sandwich, page 161) or dress a simple salad. I particularly like using it when Mediterranean ingredients and flavors are in the mix.

MAKES 2 CUPS

4 dried figs

1 cup extra-virgin olive oil

½ cup balsamic vinegar

1 teaspoon Himalayan sea salt

½ teaspoon dried Italian herb seasoning

1. In a small bowl, soak the figs in warm water for 15 minutes, until plump. Drain and reserve the soaking water.

2. In a blender, combine the olive oil, balsamic vinegar, salt, Italian herbs, soaked figs, and ¼ cup of the soaking water. Blend until smooth. Store in the fridge for up to 5 days.

CREAMY HEMPSEED RANCH DRESSING

Based on the original, of course!

MAKES 2 CUPS

1¼ cups extra-virgin olive oil

¾ cup hempseeds

¼ cup fresh lemon juice

4 garlic cloves

1 tablespoon whole black peppercorns

1 teaspoon Himalayan sea salt

¼ cup roughly chopped fresh cilantro

¼ cup roughly chopped fresh parsley

In a blender, combine the olive oil, hempseeds, lemon juice, garlic, peppercorns, salt, and ¼ cup of water and blend until smooth. Add the cilantro and parsley and blend again briefly just to incorporate. Store in the refrigerator for up to 3 days.

Adobo de Mixiote
(page 291)

Black Mole
Abuelita
(opposite)

Mole Coloradito
(page 287)

BLACK MOLE ABUELITA

This recipe was introduced to the menu by Epifanio Ruiz, one of our kitchen managers from Oaxaca, Mexico—the flavor capital of Mexico and where the rich culture of mole was born. This is his own abuelita's recipe and it has earned a place of honor on our menu. Yes, it has a number of steps to get going, but it looks like more work than it actually is. And don't let the deep roasting to the point of blackening worry you! The richness of flavor in this sauce is enhanced by the degree to which you char the ingredients. Also, note that you'll need to leave time to soak some of the ingredients for a couple of hours.

MAKES 5 CUPS

6 dried whole ancho chilies

¼ cup raw almonds

¼ cup pumpkin seeds

¼ cup raisins

6 whole raw walnuts

5 Roma tomatoes

1 corn tortilla

1 3-inch square piece of bread

1 tablespoon sesame seeds

¾ teaspoon cumin seeds

¼ cup extra-virgin olive oil

¼ cup coconut oil

½ cup sliced yellow onion

1 tablespoon finely chopped garlic

2½ teaspoons fresh thyme leaves

2 teaspoons dried thyme

2 teaspoons fresh oregano leaves

2 teaspoons Himalayan sea salt

⅛ teaspoon ground cinnamon

⅛ teaspoon whole black peppercorns

1. In a small bowl, cover 2 of the ancho chilies with warm water and soak for 2 hours. Drain, remove and discard the stems and seeds, and reserve. In another small bowl, combine the almonds, pumpkin seeds, raisins, and walnuts. Cover with 2 cups of warm water and soak for 2 hours. Drain the mixture over a small bowl to reserve the soaking liquid. Set aside.

2. Preheat the oven to 400°F.

3. Spread the tomatoes, the remaining 4 ancho chilies, the tortilla, and bread on a baking sheet. Roast in the oven until the tomatoes begin to blister and the chilies, tortilla, and bread are dry and crunchy. Everything will roast at its own pace (7 to 15 minutes), so you can use tongs to remove things to a plate as they finish. Remove and discard the stems from the chilies, roughly chop the tomatoes, and roughly tear the tortilla and bread. Set aside the tomatoes.

4. In a blender or food processor, combine the blackened chilies, toasted bread and tortilla, and the reserved soaking water from the nuts. Process until creamy and set aside.

5. Add the sesame and cumin seeds to a small, unheated pan. Gently warm the pan over medium heat until the seeds

recipe and ingredients continue

⅛ teaspoon ground cloves

¾ cup coconut sugar

½ cup chopped unsweetened dark chocolate

are golden and fragrant, about 1 minute. These can burn quickly, so transfer them immediately to a small plate and set aside to cool.

6. In a large, wide pot over medium-high, heat the olive and coconut oils together until hot but not smoking. Add the onion and garlic and cook until the onion begins to soften and become translucent, about 2 minutes. Add the soaked and drained chilies as well as the nut and seed mixture to the pot. Stir and cook for 2 minutes, then add the fresh and dried thyme, oregano, salt, cinnamon, peppercorns, and cloves plus the toasted cumin and sesame seeds. Stir, reduce the heat to medium-low, and allow the mixture to caramelize for 10 minutes, stirring occasionally.

7. Add the roasted tomatoes to the onion mixture. Cook for 5 minutes, allowing all of the ingredients to simmer together. Stir in the coconut sugar and dark chocolate and simmer for 5 more minutes.

8. Add the blended chili mixture to the pot and stir to warm everything through, about 2 minutes. Working carefully in batches, transfer the mixture to a blender or food processor and process until smooth. If you have a good immersion blender, you can do this step directly in the pot. Return the mixture to the pot and simmer, partially covered, for a final 5 minutes, until the mole is thick and glossy. Store in the refrigerator for up to 5 days.

MOLE COLORADITO

This is my favorite mole that we offer. It is very complex and savory due to the addition of the sautéed onions, sesame seeds, and roasted chilies. The ripe plaintains and raisins bring the sauce together, softening the bite of the chilies and rounding out the flavor profile in a really elegant way.

MAKES ABOUT 2 CUPS

1 tablespoon raisins

1 small dried ancho chili

1 small dried guajillo chili

1 small dried chipotle or morita chili

2 cherry tomatoes

1 garlic clove

¼ cup coconut oil

½ small yellow onion, sliced

¼ teaspoon sesame seeds

½ very ripe plantain or banana, mashed

½ teaspoon Himalayan sea salt

¼ teaspoon ground cinnamon

¼ teaspoon dried oregano

¼ teaspoon whole black peppercorns

⅛ teaspoon cumin

½ cup vegetable broth

1. In a small bowl, cover the raisins with warm water and set aside for 15 minutes.

2. In a large, wide-bottomed sauté pan or a well-seasoned cast-iron skillet over medium-high heat, toast the chilies, tomatoes, and garlic for about 5 minutes, or until they are a little charred. The tomatoes may shrivel a little and split and the chilies may look a little blackened. Remove the chili mixture to a plate and set aside.

3. In the same pan over medium heat, warm the coconut oil for 1 minute. Add the onion and sesame seeds and cook for 5 to 7 minutes, until the onion has begun to caramelize. Stir occasionally to make sure the onion doesn't stick or burn, but it'll take on better color the less it is disturbed.

4. Drain the raisins and add them, along with the mashed plantain or banana, to the onion. Continue to cook for 3 minutes, until the mixture is heated through.

5. Add the toasted chili mixture, the salt, cinnamon, oregano, peppercorns, and cumin. Cook for 2 minutes to let the flavors come together.

6. Transfer the mixture to a food processor or blender and process until smooth.

7. Return the mole to the pan over medium-low heat and stir in the vegetable broth. Reduce the heat to low and partially cover the pan. Stirring occasionally, simmer the mole for 10 to 15 minutes, until thick. Store in an airtight container in the refrigerator for up to 1 week.

RAW CACAO MOLE

This simple one-blender recipe was developed during our days as a raw-food restaurant. The ingredients are all easy to come by, and yet the combination delivers surprisingly complex flavor that rivals any mole that's been labored over for days.

MAKES 2½ CUPS

1 cup sun-dried tomatoes

½ cup fresh orange juice

¼ cup raisins

2½ tablespoons raw cacao nibs

2 tablespoons almond butter

1½ tablespoons fresh lime juice

1 garlic clove

1 tablespoon chopped red onion

1¼ teaspoons chipotle powder

¾ teaspoon Himalayan sea salt

½ teaspoon ground cumin

1. In a medium bowl, cover the sun-dried tomatoes with warm water and soak for 15 minutes. Drain the tomatoes, reserve the soaking water, and rinse.

2. In a blender, combine the soaked tomatoes, orange juice, raisins, cacao nibs, almond butter, lime juice, garlic, onion, chipotle powder, salt, and cumin. Add ½ cup of the soaking water and ½ cup of fresh water. Blend until smooth. Store in the refrigerator for up to 3 days.

GUACAMOLE

The secret to our guacamole is not overpowering the flavor of the avocados themselves. We keep it fresh and simple with just a hint of onion and garlic, and a nice, chunky texture. You don't want to overwork this so it becomes a puree.

MAKES 2 CUPS

3 avocados, cut into 1-inch cubes

3 tablespoons chopped fresh cilantro

1½ tablespoons fresh lemon juice

1½ tablespoons finely chopped red onion

1 small garlic clove, minced

1 teaspoon seeded and finely chopped jalapeño

½ teaspoon Himalayan sea salt

In a medium bowl, combine all of the ingredients. Gently mash the mixture with a potato masher, aiming for a chunky texture.

ADOBO DE MIXIOTE

This sauce and marinade comes from our endless bounty of Mexican chefs who have shared their cooking traditions with Café Gratitude. When I was having trouble sourcing organic chilies in adobo, I decided that we would make our own adobo sauce in-house. I asked around for who had a great recipe, and this has since become one of the primary marinades we use in the kitchen. It's the foundation on which our Mushroom Carnitas was built, and it gives pretty much anything a deep, smoky, irresistible flavor.

MAKES 1 CUP

2 whole dried ancho or guajillo chilies

1 Roma tomato, roughly chopped

1 red bell pepper, cored, seeded, and roughly chopped

⅓ cup chopped yellow onion

2 garlic cloves

2 dried bay or avocado leaves (see page 47)

1 whole clove

½ teaspoon whole black peppercorns

½ teaspoon dried oregano

½ teaspoon Himalayan sea salt

1. In a small bowl, cover the dried chilies with hot water. Soak for 15 minutes and drain.

2. In a blender or food processor, combine the soaked chilies, tomato, bell pepper, onion, garlic, bay leaves, clove, peppercorns, oregano, and salt. Blend until smooth. Store in the refrigerator for up to 5 days.

TOASTED ALMOND ROMESCO

A classic Spanish Romesco sauce with charred red peppers, garlic, and paprika. It's a really elegant, kind of grown-up sauce that feels like the kind of thing you'd find in a fine-dining restaurant versus a café. I find myself reaching for it to use in a number of our dishes, namely because it has a smoky, slightly fatty yumminess. It pairs particularly well with Sun-dried Tomato Pesto tossed with a simple roasted vegetable salad.

MAKES 1½ CUPS

2 medium red bell peppers

¼ cup raw almonds

2 tablespoons extra-virgin olive oil

1 teaspoon chopped garlic

1 teaspoon paprika

½ teaspoon smoked sea salt

¼ teaspoon freshly ground black pepper

⅛ teaspoon cayenne pepper

1. Over a gas flame or on a sheet pan under the broiler, char the peppers until blackened on all sides. You will be working at high heat so keep your eye on the peppers and turn them frequently to make sure they are evenly blackened. The intention is to quickly blacken the peppers, not cook them, so this process should take just a few minutes total.

2. Wrap the peppers in parchment paper and place them in a medium bowl. Cover the bowl with plastic wrap or a clean towel and leave the peppers to steam until they are cool enough to handle. Peel off and discard the charred skin and remove and discard the seeds. Strain any of the juice from the peppers and reserve for use in the sauce.

3. While the peppers cool, preheat the oven to 400°F.

4. Spread the almonds over a sheet pan and toast them in the oven for about 5 minutes, shaking the pan a couple of times so the almonds toast evenly. They should have a warm, nutty smell and be light golden on the inside.

5. Transfer the charred peppers, along with the reserved juices, and the toasted almonds to a high-speed blender. Add the olive oil, garlic, paprika, salt, black pepper, and cayenne and blend until smooth. The sauce should be thick and creamy. The density will depend on the juiciness of the peppers, and you can add up to 2 tablespoons of water to adjust the consistency. Store in the refrigerator in a covered container for up to 5 days.

GREMOLATA

Because of the fresh bits of garlic and parsley and the tang from the lemon zest, this has become my go-to garnish for a number of Café Gratitude dishes. Even though it's primarily an Italian preparation, we use it for Mexican and even Indian preparations. It brightens up the flavors of just about anything you put it on.

MAKES ABOUT 1 CUP

1 bunch fresh flat-leaf Italian parsley, leaves picked and stems discarded

One 2-inch piece of lemon peel

1 garlic clove

⅛ teaspoon Himalayan sea salt

1. Pile the parsley leaves, lemon peel, garlic, and salt on a cutting board and chop them all together, mixing and turning as you go, until the texture is fine and sprinkleable.

2. Store in the refrigerator for up to 2 days.

NOTE It is important that these ingredients are chopped together (as opposed to chopping separately and then mixing) so that all of the oils of each ingredient come together. But be careful not to over-chop! The result should be an aromatic herb mixture that you can easily sprinkle as a garnish.

Guacamole
(page 289)

Mole Coloradito
(page 287)

Roasted
Tomatillo
Sauce
(opposite)

Goji Chipotle
Dressing
(page 278)

ROASTED TOMATILLO SAUCE

We make this sauce in the high summer when tomatillos are in season. It's used in a number of applications where we want some acid and smokiness, though it has a definitive Mexican feel. You can make this sauce completely creamy, but we leave it with just a little texture so you get the nice little flecks of the tomatillo seeds.

MAKES 3 CUPS

2 pounds tomatillos, husked

1 Roma tomato

2 garlic cloves

1 whole dried chipotle pepper

1½ teaspoons Himalayan sea salt

1. Preheat the oven to 450°F.

2. Arrange the tomatillos, tomato, and garlic cloves on a baking sheet. Roast until the tomatillo skins are starting to char and the tomato has split and begun to give up its juice, checking every couple of minutes for about 15 minutes. Set aside to cool.

3. Transfer the cooled mixture to a blender with the dried chipotle and salt. Blend until smooth yet keeping the chipotle seeds intact. The sauce should be slightly thick and viscous, so depending on the density of the tomatillos, you may need to add a little water (up to ¼ cup) to create the desired consistency. Store in the refrigerator for up to 5 days.

ADOBO BUFFALO SAUCE

All the spicy, pepper-forward flavor of the classic sauce but made fresh and with vegan butter. Miyoko's European Style Cultured Vegan Butter is my vegan butter of choice because it has only whole-food ingredients and the taste is amazing. But there are other vegan butters on the market that will also work just fine in this recipe.

MAKES 3 CUPS

3 whole dried ancho or guajillo chilies

2 small Roma tomatoes, roughly chopped

1 red bell pepper, cored, seeded, and chopped

½ cup chopped yellow onion

3 garlic cloves

½ teaspoon Himalayan sea salt

½ teaspoon black peppercorns

½ teaspoon dried oregano

¼ teaspoon cayenne pepper

3 dried avocado leaves (see page 47) or bay leaves

1 whole clove

½ cup Miyoko's European Style Cultured Vegan Butter

½ cup apple cider vinegar

1. In a medium bowl, soak the dried chilies in warm water until soft, about 1 hour.

2. Drain the chilies, remove and discard their stems and seeds, and transfer them to a high-speed blender. Add the tomatoes, bell pepper, onion, garlic, salt, peppercorns, oregano, cayenne, avocado leaves, and clove. Blend the ingredients into a smooth sauce.

3. In a medium skillet over medium-high heat, heat the vegan butter until it is melted and simmering. Add the apple cider vinegar, and once it is heated through, add the sauce mixture and bring to a rolling simmer. Keep the sauce at an active simmer for 5 to 7 minutes, until it is reduced by a third or begins to thicken slightly.

4. Cover and refrigerate for up to 3 days.

SALSA VERDE

We call upon this classic Mexican sauce for a number of our dishes—drizzled over chilaquiles, slathered in a burrito, or as a dip for chips. We frequently pair it up with Roasted Tomatillo Sauce (page 295) and Cashew Crema (page 311) for the signature Mexican red, white, and green combination.

MAKES 2 CUPS

1 avocado

1 large jalapeño, seeded and roughly chopped

1 bunch fresh cilantro, leaves only

3 scallions (white and green parts), chopped

¼ cup fresh lemon juice

1 large garlic clove, chopped

½ teaspoon Himalayan sea salt

¼ teaspoon freshly ground black pepper

In a blender, combine the avocado, jalapeño, cilantro, scallions, lemon juice, garlic, salt, pepper, and 1 cup of water. Blend until smooth. Store in the refrigerator for up to 3 days.

RAW ZUCCHINI CILANTRO HUMMUS

Aside from having super bright flavor thanks to the zucchini and fresh cilantro, we love this recipe because it doesn't require any of the usual prep that comes with having to cook chickpeas. It's light, bright, and completely raw. We keep ours on the slightly chunky side because we like to see the texture of the ingredients, but it's also beautiful blended up into more of a traditional creamy consistency, as in the recipe here.

MAKES 2 CUPS

1 cup roughly chopped zucchini

1 cup sunflower seeds, soaked for 2 hours, drained, and rinsed

¼ cup roughly chopped fresh cilantro leaves and stems

2½ tablespoons fresh lemon juice

2 teaspoons sesame tahini

1 teaspoon chopped garlic

½ teaspoon ground cumin

½ teaspoon Himalayan sea salt

¼ teaspoon freshly ground black pepper

¼ teaspoon cayenne

⅓ cup extra-virgin olive oil

In a food processor, combine the zucchini, sunflower seeds, cilantro, lemon juice, tahini, garlic, cumin, salt, black pepper, and cayenne and process until combined and almost uniform. With the food processor running, stream in the olive oil and blend until smooth. Store in the refrigerator for up to 3 days.

SESAME WASABI SAUCE

This is essentially a Japanese vinaigrette, which we use on our Asian-inspired bowls and salads. The wasabi gives it nice zing without being overwhelming, while the toasted sesame oil creates a beautiful round flavor. It pairs especially nicely if you add a seaweed element to a salad.

MAKES 2 CUPS

½ cup plus 2 tablespoons fresh orange juice

½ cup brown rice vinegar

¼ cup tamari

¼ jalapeño, seeded

1 tablespoon sesame tahini

1 tablespoon toasted sesame oil

2 teaspoons fresh ginger juice or one 1-inch knob fresh ginger

1½ teaspoons wasabi powder

1½ teaspoons Himalayan sea salt

½ cup extra-virgin olive oil

In a blender, combine the orange juice, vinegar, tamari, jalapeño, tahini, sesame oil, ginger, wasabi, and salt and blend on high speed until smooth. Lower the speed to medium and slowly stream in the olive oil, allowing the dressing to emulsify. Store in the refrigerator for up to 5 days.

QUESTION *of the day* / What human qualities do you most admire?

Sun-dried Tomato
Pesto
(page 303)

Cilantro
Pumpkin Seed Pesto
(opposite)

Basil Hempseed
Pesto
(page 302)

CILANTRO PUMPKIN SEED PESTO

Our twist on the more commonly known basil pesto. The fattiness of the pumpkin seeds rounds out the herbiness of the cilantro, giving it a flavor that works really well with both Mexican- and Spanish-inspired dishes. It pairs beautifully with the Toasted Almond Romesco sauce (page 292), especially spooned over a roasted cauliflower steak or fried squash blossoms.

MAKES 2 CUPS

2¼ cups chopped fresh cilantro

¾ cup raw pumpkin seeds

1 small jalapeño or serrano pepper, seeded and chopped

1 garlic clove, chopped

1 tablespoon plus 2 teaspoons fresh lime juice

¾ teaspoon Himalayan sea salt

½ cup extra-virgin olive oil

In a food processor, combine the cilantro, pumpkin seeds, jalapeño or serrano pepper, garlic, lime juice, and salt. Pulse until the ingredients are well chopped but still maintain some texture. With the food processor running, slowly drizzle in the olive oil and process until emulsified. Store in the refrigerator for up to 1 week.

BASIL HEMPSEED PESTO

Our perennial summertime favorite. This version is nut-free and uses hempseeds as the nutty, fatty component. Otherwise it's fairly traditional and can be used on everything from salads to grain bowls, sandwiches to pastas.

MAKES 1 CUP

2 cups lightly packed fresh basil, leaves only

½ cup extra-virgin olive oil, plus more if needed

½ cup hempseeds

1 teaspoon chopped garlic

½ teaspoon Himalayan sea salt

Combine the basil, olive oil, hempseeds, garlic, and sea salt in a food processor and process until smooth. If not serving immediately, cover with a thin layer of olive oil to prevent discoloration and store in an airtight container in the refrigerator for 3 to 5 days.

QUESTION *of the day* / What would love to do now?

SUN-DRIED TOMATO PESTO

This is our winter version of the use-everywhere Basil Hempseed Pesto. The pistachios give this a deep, rich flavor that's complemented by the tomatoes and brightened by a bit of preserved lemon.

MAKES 2 CUPS

1 cup sun-dried tomatoes

½ cup hempseeds

¼ cup raw pistachios

1½ tablespoons chopped preserved lemon peel or freshly grated lemon zest

1½ tablespoons chopped fresh herbs, such as rosemary, thyme, parsley, or marjoram (any ratio of your preference)

2 teaspoons Basil Hempseed Pesto (page 302)

2 teaspoons chopped garlic

1 teaspoon smoked salt

Extra-virgin olive oil, if needed

1. In a medium bowl, cover the sun-dried tomatoes with hot water and let them soak for 15 minutes. Drain and reserve the soaking water.

2. In a food processor, combine the soaked sun-dried tomatoes, hempseeds, pistachios, lemon peel, herbs, basil hempseed pesto, garlic, salt, and 2 tablespoons of the tomato soaking water. Process until smooth, adding a tablespoon or 2 more soaking water if needed to loosen the mixture. If not using immediately, cover with a thin layer of olive oil to prevent discoloration and store in an airtight container in the refrigerator for 3 to 5 days.

SPICY TOMATO JAM

Another one of our chameleon sauces, this condiment would be just as at home on an Indian dish as a chutney as it would be on an antipasto platter with nut cheeses or a Middle Eastern or Mediterranean plate with falafel.

MAKES 4 CUPS

1 tablespoon cumin seeds

½ cup finely chopped fresh ginger

½ cup apple cider vinegar

¼ cup chopped whole lemons

4 pounds Roma tomatoes, diced

1½ cups cane sugar

1½ cups coconut sugar

1 tablespoon ground cinnamon

1 teaspoon ground cloves

1 teaspoon Himalayan sea salt

1 teaspoon cayenne pepper

1. In a small pan over medium heat, toast the cumin seeds until they are fragrant, occasionally shaking the pan, about 3 minutes.

2. In a blender, combine the toasted cumin seeds, ginger, apple cider vinegar, and lemon and blend until the mixture is well chopped. Set aside.

3. In large, heavy-bottomed saucepan over medium-high heat, combine the tomatoes, cane sugar, coconut sugar, cinnamon, cloves, salt, and cayenne. Stir in the blended ginger-lemon mixture and bring everything to a boil.

4. While you are waiting for the tomato jam to come to a boil, pop a small plate into your freezer. You will need this to test the gelling point of the jam.

5. Keep the mixture at a rolling boil until the tomatoes cook down to a jam-like consistency and the sugars are caramelized, about 25 minutes. As the jam reduces, be sure to stir it so the jam doesn't burn on the bottom.

6. When you think the jam looks ready, remove the plate from the freezer and put a tablespoon of jam on it. Return the plate to the freezer for 1 minute. If after that minute the jam stays nice and firm or moves very little when you tip the plate sideways, you know it is ready. If it is still runny, it needs a little more time to cook down.

7. Allow the spicy tomato jam to cool before serving. Store the jam in a large jar (or several small jars) in the refrigerator, where it will keep for up to 2 weeks.

MINT-COCONUT CHUTNEY

A great nondairy alternative to yogurt-based chutneys. Here we use coconut meat, which gives the condiment a beautiful, rich creaminess that's brightened by the mint. It's a great way to lighten up any Indian-inspired dish.

MAKES 3½ CUPS

½ cup roughly chopped white onion

½ cup shredded or flaked unsweetened coconut

¼ cup young-Thai coconut meat, fresh (see page 33) or frozen and thawed

¼ cup fresh lemon juice

½ to 1 small jalapeño, seeded

1½ teaspoons Himalayan sea salt

1 teaspoon chopped fresh ginger

1 cup chopped fresh cilantro leaves

½ cup chopped fresh mint leaves

In a blender, combine the onion, shredded coconut, fresh coconut, lemon juice, jalapeño, salt, and ginger with 1 cup of water. Blend on high speed until the mixture is smooth and creamy. Add the chopped cilantro and mint and continue blending on low speed, or pulse if your blender has that capability, until the leaves are broken down. You still want to see green flecks of herb in your chutney, so be careful not to overblend. Store in the refrigerator for up to 5 days.

SPICY COCKTAIL SAUCE/ CHIPOTLE KETCHUP

This is a rich condiment that's fantastically versatile as both a cocktail sauce and ketchup stand-in. It also makes a really nice chipotle aioli when blended with the Cashew Nacho Cheese (page 314). If you are using this as a ketchup, make sure that you take the time to really reduce the recipe so that your sauce is satisfyingly thickened.

MAKES 2 CUPS

2 tablespoons extra-virgin olive oil

½ cup diced red onion

⅓ cup diced fennel

½ stalk celery, roughly chopped

One 1½-inch knob fresh ginger

½ teaspoon chipotle powder

1 garlic clove

1½ teaspoons coriander seeds

½ teaspoon Himalayan sea salt

½ teaspoon freshly ground black pepper

⅛ teaspoon ground cloves

4 cups chopped fresh tomatoes

½ cup lightly packed fresh basil, stems and leaves, roughly chopped

⅓ cup apple cider vinegar

2½ tablespoons coconut sugar

1. In a large sauté pan, heat the olive oil over medium heat. Add the onion, fennel, celery, ginger, chipotle powder, garlic, coriander seeds, salt, pepper, and ground cloves. Cook until the vegetables are soft, about 10 minutes. Add the tomatoes and 2 cups of water and cook until the mixture is reduced by half, about 20 minutes.

2. Transfer the mixture to a blender, add the basil, and blend until smooth. Return the mixture to the pan over medium-high heat. Stir in the apple cider vinegar and coconut sugar and reduce until the sauce is nice and thick, 20 to 25 minutes. If you're making cocktail sauce, you can err on a little less time for a thinner sauce. If you're making ketchup and you want to get the sauce extra smooth, pass it through a fine-mesh strainer. Allow the sauce to cool and store in the refrigerator for up to 1 week.

BARBECUE SAUCE

This classic BBQ sauce has a number of ingredients but they are all easy to source and it is pretty much a one-pot stop.

MAKES 3 CUPS

½ pound Roma tomatoes, cut into large cubes

¼ pound peaches, fresh or frozen, cubed

1 whole dried chipotle pepper

¼ cup apple cider vinegar

2½ tablespoons roughly chopped white onion

2½ tablespoons sun-dried tomatoes, rehydrated in hot water to cover for 10 minutes, drained, and chopped

2½ tablespoons coconut sugar

2 tablespoons white wine

1 tablespoon tamarind paste or 1 Medjool date, pitted

1 tablespoon molasses

2 teaspoons smoked sea salt

1½ teaspoons capers in brine, drained

1 garlic clove

½ teaspoon liquid smoke

3 whole black peppercorns

⅛ teaspoon yellow mustard seeds

⅛ teaspoon paprika

1. In a large, heavy-bottomed pot over medium-high heat, combine all of the ingredients. Cook for 10 to 12 minutes, until the tomatoes start to break down, stirring frequently to prevent the sauce from sticking to the bottom of the pot. Partially cover the pot and reduce the heat to low, keeping the mixture at a slow boil for 15 to 20 more minutes. Once the tomatoes and peaches have broken down and the juices have begun to thicken, remove the pot from the heat. Remove the lid and allow the sauce to cool for 5 minutes.

2. Working in batches, carefully transfer the sauce to a blender or food processor and blend until smooth.

3. Rinse out the pot to remove any leftover bits that didn't make it to the blender and return the blended sauce to the pot. If you want a superfine sauce, which I love, pass the blended sauce through a fine-mesh strainer first. If you like a more rustic sauce, you can skip this step.

4. Over low heat, bring the sauce to a simmer, stirring frequently until it is thick and glossy, about 10 minutes. The sauce will likely bubble and spit as it reduces. You can keep the pot partially covered between stirs and use a long-handled spoon to protect yourself from spatters. The sauce will keep for at least 10 days covered in the refrigerator.

CHEESES & PICKLED THINGS

Cashew Ricotta
(opposite)

Cashew Mozzarella balls
(page 312)

Cashew
Mozzarella
(page 312)

Brazil Nut
Parmesan
(page 317)

CASHEW CREMA/RICOTTA

This is a great basic vegan pantry sauce because you can use it as a tangy, heavy cream-like drizzle on pretty much anything. We finish our pizzas with it to give them a mozzarella cheese look and feel, stir it into sauces for extra body and a slight lemony flavor, and drape it over pastas like a melted soft cheese. Depending on how we're using it, we either refer to it as "crema" or "ricotta."

MAKES ABOUT 1 CUP

½ cup raw cashews, soaked for at least 2 hours and up to 8 hours

2 tablespoons fresh lemon juice

¼ teaspoon Himalayan sea salt

Drain and rinse the cashews and transfer them to a high-speed blender. Add the lemon juice and salt along with ½ cup of water. Blend until smooth and creamy. Refrigerate in an airtight container for up to 5 days.

CASHEW MOZZARELLA

This is a very easy nut cheese to make, but it requires a little forethought, as you will need to soak both the Irish moss and cashews at least 8 hours in advance and refrigerate the cheese for 4 hours to set up. You will also need a high-speed blender to properly break down the Irish moss and fully blend the cheese. If you'd like the cheese to have a dense, feta-like consistency, set it in the freezer for 10 to 15 minutes before serving. Otherwise, the cheese will have a softer, creamier consistency. You can't go wrong either way!

MAKES 1 CUP

¾ ounce Irish moss (see Note)

¾ teaspoon Himalayan sea salt

½ cup raw cashews, soaked for 8 hours, drained, and rinsed

¼ cup coconut oil, melted

1. Carefully wash the moss, as it can often be very sandy from the harvest. In a large bowl, cover the moss with abundant cold water and let it soak in the fridge for at least 8 hours. (Allow extra room in your soaking container, as the Irish moss will expand with water as it soaks.) Don't rinse the moss after the soaking process is complete. You can keep soaked Irish moss covered in the fridge for up to 1 month; just make sure not to drain or replace the soaking water.

2. Shake off any extra water from the moss and weigh it using a digital scale to make sure you have exactly 1 ounce. Roughly chop the moss.

3. In a high-speed blender, combine the moss, salt, and ¼ cup of water. Blend on medium speed until the moss begins to create a thick jelly. Small bits of moss may accumulate on the sides of the blender or under the lid, so stop to scrape them down using a spatula. If the mixture is too thick to be blended into a smooth jelly, you can add a small amount of additional water. Make sure the mixture is completely smooth; otherwise you will have small bits of moss in your cheese that will be impossible to eliminate.

4. Add the cashews and coconut oil and blend on medium-high speed. Using the blender plunger or a spatula, work the mixture pretty aggressively so that it becomes smooth and creamy. I'm not going to lie, you will have to work this cheese. You can add a small amount of water if the going gets tough, but don't give up until you have a smooth mixture, about 1 minute. It will be worth it!

5. Pour the cashew mozzarella into a small jar or other lidded container, cover, and refrigerate for at least 4 hours to set up. The mozzarella will keep for up to 5 days in the fridge.

NOTE Irish moss is seaweed. Most often it is used as a vegan gelatin or thickener in recipes and is purported to have many health benefits. We have used Irish moss since we opened Café Gratitude, primarily in our raw cakes, creams, and cheeses, because it is versatile and does not require heat to activate its gelling properties. While it might be difficult to find at your local supermarket, Irish moss can be easily sourced online. For this recipe, you will need to purchase the whole seaweed, not the flakes.

VARIATION Once the cashew mozzarella has set up, you can serve this cheese as soft cream cheese or play with alternate presentations. It is delicious formed into small bocconcini and rolled in cracked black peppercorns (see photo on page 310).

Additionally, you can roll the mozzarella in a sheet of baker's parchment to create a cylinder and garnish with chopped pistachio or freshly chopped herbs (photos on pages 92 and 95).

CASHEW NACHO CHEESE

When we created this creamy cheese, we gained a kitchen staple that is so versatile that it can be used in almost any dish in which a creamy, spicy punch is called for. We have used it as a nacho-style sauce in our Mexican grain bowls, a spicy aioli on our Mediterranean-inspired chickpea frittata, and as a dipping sauce with the Buffalo Cauliflower (see page 113)—it always feels right at home.

MAKES 3 CUPS

1 cup raw cashews, soaked for 4 hours

2 tablespoons raw pumpkin seeds, ground

½ to 1 jalapeño, seeded

2 tablespoons fresh lemon juice

1 small garlic clove

1½ teaspoons Himalayan sea salt

1½ teaspoons chipotle powder

Drain and rinse the cashews under cold water until the water runs clear. Transfer the cashews to a blender and add the ground pumpkin seeds, jalapeño, lemon juice, garlic, salt, and chipotle powder with 1¼ cups of water. Blend until the cheese is smooth and creamy. Store covered in the refrigerator for up to 4 days.

CASHEW CRÈME FRAICHE

This fermented crème is best made 2 to 3 days prior to use and can be kept in the refrigerator for at least a week. The coconut kefir acts as the fermentation element and the longer you let the crème sit, the tangier it gets.

MAKES ABOUT 1 CUP

¾ cup raw cashews, soaked for at least 2 hours and up to 8 hours

½ cup plus 2 tablespoons coconut kefir

2 tablespoons fresh lemon juice

1 teaspoon Himalayan sea salt

Drain and rinse the cashews under running water until the water runs clear. Transfer them to a blender and add the coconut kefir, lemon juice, and salt. Blend until completely smooth and store covered in the refrigerator for up to 1 week.

QUESTION *of the day* / How can you be courageous today?

MACADAMIA CHEDDAR

This simple nut cheese also makes an amazing Kraft-style mac 'n' cheese. Just toss the cheese with your freshly cooked pasta of choice, incorporating a little of the cooking water from the pasta, and you're good to go!

MAKES 2 CUPS

2 small red bell peppers, cored, seeded, and roughly chopped

2 tablespoons fresh lemon juice

1 teaspoon Himalayan sea salt

1½ cups raw macadamia nuts

In a high-speed blender, combine the peppers, lemon juice, and salt and blend until smooth. Add the nuts and, using the blender plunger or a spatula, blend on high speed until you have a smooth, homogenous mixture. If necessary, pause to scrape down the sides of the blender with a spatula. The cheese will be dense and the consistency will depend on how much juice the bell peppers contain. You may need to add a tablespoon of water or 2 to help the blending process, but be careful not to overdo it. Store covered in the refrigerator for up to 5 days.

BRAZIL NUT PARMESAN

This selenium-rich garlicky crumble is a perfect topping wherever you would use traditional Parmesan, as well as over a savory breakfast porridge.

MAKES 2 CUPS

2 cups whole Brazil nuts

2 teaspoons finely chopped garlic

½ teaspoon Himalayan sea salt

Combine the nuts, garlic, and salt in a food processor and pulse until you have a light, fluffy crumble. Be careful not to overprocess, as the oil in the Brazil nuts will turn it into a paste. Store covered in the refrigerator for up to 1 week.

QUESTION *of the day* / Who could you reach out to and include today?

ESCABECHE

I would honestly say that our *escabeche*—lightly cooked vegetables that are pickled in a vinegar-forward brine—is one of the best I've ever had. It's perhaps more complex than what you'd find in a taqueria, but the result is deeply flavored and delicious. One thing to note is that you do not want to overcook the vegetables; they should be nice and crisp without being raw, and even then you're only blanching the sturdier, starchier vegetables. The more delicate ones will "cook" in the pickling brine. Also, be careful to not use red onion or beets, as they'll stain the mixture pink.

MAKES 4 CUPS

2 teaspoons extra-virgin olive oil

1 dried bay leaf

1 small cinnamon stick

1 star anise

½ teaspoon cumin seeds

½ teaspoon whole black peppercorns

½ teaspoon dried thyme

½ teaspoon dried oregano

½ teaspoon red chili flakes

½ cup ½-inch-thick slices yellow onion

1 garlic clove, smashed

2 cups apple cider vinegar

1½ teaspoons Himalayan sea salt, plus more if blanching the vegetables

1½ teaspoons coconut sugar

4 cups mixed vegetables cut into bite-sized pieces, such as baby zucchini, baby carrots, bell peppers, celery, broccoli, or cauliflower

¼ to ½ of a jalapeño, seeded and sliced into ¼-inch-thick rounds

1. Warm the olive oil in a medium pot over medium heat. Add the bay leaf, cinnamon stick, star anise, cumin seeds, peppercorns, thyme, oregano, and chili flakes and toast in the oil for 2 minutes, until the spices are warm and fragrant.

2. Add the onion and garlic and sauté until the onion is slightly softened, about 3 minutes. Add the apple cider vinegar and 2 cups of water and bring the mixture to a boil. Add the salt and coconut sugar and stir to dissolve. Remove the pot from the heat and allow the mixture to cool for 5 minutes.

3. If you're using any broccoli and/or cauliflower, fill a large pot with salted water and bring to a boil. Add the broccoli and cook for 3 minutes or until it's just barely tender but still retains some crunch. Drain the vegetables.

4. In a large lidded jar or covered container, combine all of the vegetables and the jalapeño. Pour the vinegar-onion mixture over the vegetables, adding a little more water if necessary to top off the jar and keep the vegetables submerged. Cover tightly and store in the refrigerator. The vegetables will need to pickle overnight before serving and will keep in the refrigerator for up to 2 weeks.

PURPLE CABBAGE KIMCHI

The kimchi that we serve at Café Gratitude isn't in the traditional Korean style now familiar to many people but is rather a beautiful spicy (purple) cabbage and daikon sauerkraut. It is fun and interesting to make your own kimchi or sauerkraut, especially because you can store it in the refrigerator for up to 3 months and use it for all manner of things, from tossing it into salads to stirring it into hot vegetable dishes. If you have a ceramic crock specially designed for making sauerkraut, that is ideal, but you can also make kimchi in a large stainless-steel saucepan with great results. In addition to a large container for the kimchi, you will need a plate that fits inside of the container that you will use to hold the kimchi under the brine while it's fermenting. Another useful tool would be an 8-cup Mason jar with a lid that you can fill with water and use as a weight to maintain pressure on top of the plate. You don't need to get too fancy or complicated; this is the food of peasants!

MAKES 2 QUARTS

1 large head of red cabbage, cored and shredded (see Note)

½ pound daikon radish, shredded (see Note)

2 tablespoons coarse sea salt (we like La Baleine), plus more to taste

½ cup seeded and roughly chopped jalapeños

2 tablespoons chopped garlic cloves

1. In a large bowl, combine the cabbage, daikon, and 2 tablespoons of the salt. Using your hands, vigorously massage the vegetables. You want to break down the cell walls of the cabbage and daikon a little so that they begin to release their juices. When you feel the mixture has started to become moist, let it rest for 15 minutes at room temperature, then taste to check the salt level. The vegetables should taste salty but not overwhelmingly. Trust your palate, but remember that the salt will keep your vegetables nice and crunchy. If you go too light, you run the risk of your vegetables becoming soft as they ferment. If you feel like it's too salty, you can take out a portion of the vegetables and rinse away the salt using a colander. Make sure you eliminate excess water before returning the vegetables to the bowl.

2. Fold in the jalapeños and garlic. Then, using your fist or a kitchen mallet, pack the vegetables tightly into your fermentation container. The more you bruise the cabbage as you go, the more juice it will release, so really go for it! Pour over any salty juice from the bottom of the bowl, cover the vegetables with a plate, and use a water-filled Mason jar to

weigh it down. Scrape down the sides of the container so there are no pieces of cabbage or daikon above the liquid level. Check again in a couple of hours to make sure the cabbage is completely submerged. If not, boil some water, allow it to cool, and add it to the container to cover the cabbage mixture.

3. Cover the fermentation container with a large dish towel and secure it with kitchen twine or a rubber band to keep out any insects while the cabbage is fermenting. Set the kimchi in a cool, dark corner of your house and let it ferment for 3 to 10 days. Fermentation is a very individual process and will depend a lot on your environmental conditions. Heat will speed up the process and cold will slow it down. After 3 days, check the kimchi daily to see what it tastes like. Remove any small bits of mold that might grow on the surface. This is normal and won't affect the cabbage. When you feel that the kimchi has the bite and texture you are looking for, transfer it to a clean jar and keep it in the refrigerator for up to 3 months.

NOTE You can shred the cabbage and daikon using a mandoline, a food processor with a shredding blade, or even by hand, which I find easiest and most enjoyable when I am making this recipe at home.

PICKLED BEETS

When we first developed our blue plate special, it made me think about my own holiday dinners growing up. Pickled beets were always on my table, and this is a classic grandma recipe. Just take care not to overcook the beets or they will get mushy.

MAKES 4 CUPS

4 medium beets, scrubbed

1 cup apple cider vinegar

½ cup cane sugar

1½ teaspoons whole cloves

1½ teaspoons whole allspice

½ teaspoon Himalayan sea salt

1. In a large pot over high heat, combine the beets with enough water to cover them. Bring the water to a boil, reduce the heat to a healthy simmer, and cook the beets until they can be pierced with a small, sharp knife, 20 to 30 minutes. Cooking time will vary depending on the size of your beets.

2. Drain the beets and set aside until they are cool enough to handle. Once cooled, peel the beets and cut them into wedges. Place the wedges in a large jar or bowl.

3. In a medium saucepan over medium-high heat, combine the apple cider vinegar, sugar, cloves, allspice, and salt. Bring the mixture to a boil and boil for 5 minutes. Pour the pickling mixture over the beet wedges. Allow to marinate at least 2 hours before serving. These will keep covered and refrigerated for up to 2 weeks.

BISTRO PICKLED CARROTS

This recipe works best when you can find thin, market-fresh baby carrots that are approximately ¼ inch in diameter and less than 5 inches in length, but you can also use slightly larger carrots and cut them down to size.

MAKES 2 POUNDS OF PICKLED CARROTS

2 pounds baby carrots

2 cups apple cider vinegar

2 garlic cloves

2 teaspoons Himalayan sea salt

2 teaspoons coriander seeds

1 teaspoon whole black peppercorns

1 teaspoon caraway seeds

1 dried bay leaf

1. Wash the carrots to remove any dirt. Trim the stem ends but do not peel the carrots. Set aside and prepare the brine.

2. In a large saucepan over medium-high heat, combine the apple cider vinegar, garlic, salt, coriander, peppercorns, caraway seeds, and bay leaf with 2 cups of water and bring to a boil. Allow the mixture to boil for 3 minutes. Add the carrots and boil for an additional 2 minutes. Remove the pan from the heat and let the brine cool completely at room temperature. You may also transfer the carrots and the brine to a storage container and let them cool in the refrigerator. Store the pickled carrots with their brine in a covered container in the refrigerator for up to 1 month. They will be ready to enjoy in just a couple of hours, though they're better if left overnight.

ACKNOWLEDGMENTS

FROM Dreux Ellis

We are all interdependent, so this cookbook and what I have created with Café Gratitude is a reflection of my "interbeing" with so many people whom I would like to acknowledge and thank from the bottom of my heart:

Matthew and Terces Engelhart, meeting you was a profound turning point in my life. You are pioneers in the awakening of love, and your commitment to the founding principles of Café Gratitude—in good times and in adversity—has inspired me profoundly.

Cary Moiser and Ryland Engelhart, for continuing to forge the path that your parents so bravely pioneered, and with the same dedication and truthfulness.

Lisa Bonbright, for your persistence of vision. Your energy and commitment to excellence have been a foundation of our success. Thank you for your partnership and the unlimited platform you created for my work.

To the city of Venice and my Italian family and friends who welcomed me into their lives and nurtured my budding dream of becoming a chef. Per Angelo Carbone, *per sempre, e per la mia grande maestra Maddalena Salzone. Per Susanna Morasco e Martina Trois, la mia famiglia italiana, grazie per tutto quello che mi avete insegnato e l'amore e la fiducia che mi avete dato. Ringrazio anche Doriana Presotto per avermi dato il mio primo lavoro come Chef e per la sua amicizia.*

Chandra Gilbert and Alice Liu, dear friends and colleagues whose love and friendship has sustained me on this path with Café Gratitude and the incredibly dedicated and hard-working "Heart of the House" teams who have fed many thousands of meals to our guests over the years. Special thanks to Beto Roque, Jaime Salinas, and Hugo Alquicira for your assistance on recipe testing and food styling on this cookbook.

A very special acknowledgment to Tiziana Alipo Tamborra and Matthew Rogers for their enduring recipes that have been the foundation of our Cafe Gratitude Classic raw desserts and to Isamar Curiel Santos and Sergio Mendez, who have built on this foundation.

Thank you, Isamar and Sergio, for your exciting new desserts and all of the inspiration and dedication you have brought to the process of creating this cookbook.

Lisa Romerein, Rebecca Farr and Robin Turk, whose beautiful photographs have made our food look so enticing in these pages. Such a pleasure to work with all of you.

Nicole Tourtelot and Lucia Watson, for believing in this book and giving us the opportunity to share these recipes and our version of a grateful life with the world outside of Southern California. You have made the process of creating a first cookbook so rewarding and fun.

Rachel Holtzman, for your warm and generous encouragement, intuitive understanding, and grounded authenticity.

My parents, Sharon and Aberhard Jaeck, for their constant support and encouragement. What I have created here is a reflection of your job well done.

My Zen teacher, Abbess Furyu Nancy Schroeder of Green Gulch Farm, who has given me wise counsel and much laughter over the past eight years while gently nudging me into the present.

Finally to my Kurichan, Chris Perez, who inspires me daily, keeps me in my practice, and moves me from my head into my heart.

FROM Lisa Bonbright / I would like to echo each of Dreux's sentiments, and add a few heartfelt thank-yous of my own:

To Matthew and Terces Engelhart, for giving the world Café Gratitude, and allowing me to share in that gift.

To TableArt in Los Angeles, for helping us make this book as special and as beautiful as I'd always imagined it could be.

To Mark Lehman, for your unyielding support and guidance.

To Paris and Eden, who inspire me every day to follow my dreams and be true to myself. Without their thumbs-up at our first Café Gratitude tasting, we wouldn't be where we are today.

And to Chris Bonbright. Thank you for helping me follow my heart; the world has more love in it because of you.

We wish to express our thanks to TableArt, a truly unique boutique in Los Angeles, and its owner, Walter Lowry. TableArt loaned many pieces for this book, including dinnerware by small, difficult-to-find producers such as Christiane Perrochon, Potomak Studio, DBO Home, Jan Burtz, and Haand—to name just a few. We are very grateful for their participation in this project and encourage our community to seek out and support their many artists at www.tableartonline.com.

INDEX

Note: Page numbers in *italics* indicate photos.